The Royal Court Theatre presents

D0596679

The Weir

by Conor McPherson

First performance at the Royal Court Theatre Upstairs 4 July 1997.

The Royal Court Theatre is financially assisted by the Royal Borough of Kensington and Chelsea. Recipient of a grant from the Theatre Restoration Fund & from the Foundation for Sport & the Arts. The Royal Court's Play Development Programme is funded by the Audrey Skirball-Kenis Theatre. Supported by the National Lottery through the Arts Council of England. Royal Court Registered Charity number 231242.

How the Royal Court is brought to you

The Royal Court (English Stage Company Ltd) is supported financially by a wide range of public bodies and private companies, as well as its own trading activities. The company receives its principal funding from the **Arts Council of England**, which has supported the Royal Court since 1956. The **Royal Borough of Kensington & Chelsea** gives an annual grant to the Royal Court Young People's Theatre. The **London Boroughs Grants Committee** contributes to the cost of productions in the Theatre Upstairs.

Other parts of the company's activities are made possible by business sponsorships. Several of these sponsors have made a long-term commitment. 1996 saw the sixth Barclays New Stages Festival of Independent Theatre, supported throughout by **Barclays Bank**. **British Gas North Thames** supported three years of the Royal Court's Education Programme. Sponsorship by **WH Smith** helped to make the launch of the Friends of the Royal Court scheme so successful.

1993 saw the start of our association with the **Audrey Skirball-Kenis Theatre** of Los Angeles, which is funding a Playwrights Programme at the Royal Court. Exchange visits for writers between Britain and the USA complement the greatly increased programme of readings and workshops which have fortified the company's capability to develop new plays.

In 1988 the **Olivier Building Appeal** was launched, to raise funds to begin the task of restoring, repairing and improving the Royal Court Theatre, Sloane Square. This was made possible by a large number of generous supporters and significant contributions from the **Theatres Restoration Fund**, the **Rayne Foundation**, the **Foundation for Sport and the Arts** and the **Arts Council's Incentive Funding Scheme**.

The Company earns the rest of the money it needs to operate from the Box Office, from other trading and from transfers to the West End of plays such as **Death and the Maiden**, **Six Degrees of Separation**, **Oleanna** and **My Night With Reg**. But without public subsidy it would close immediately and its unique place in British theatre would be lost.

he Royal Court has a track record of success; I am
ssociated with it because it is uniquely placed to
ke advantage of the current climate of optimism,
nergy and innovation.

ur plans for the transformed theatre in Sloane
quare include the latest stage technology, a cafe
ar and improved audience facilities enabling us to
nticipate the latest in contemporary drama whilst at
e same time the refurbished building will bear
stimony to our past successes.

invite you to become part of these exciting plans.

erry Robinson
hairman, Granada Group

you would like more information please contact me
t the Royal Court Theatre, St Martin's Lane, London
VC2N 4BG.

The Royal Court Theatre,
Sloane Square, was built in
1888 and is the longest-
established theatre in
England with the dedicated
aim of producing new plays.
We were thrilled to be
awarded £16.2 million in
September 1995 - from the

National Lottery through the Arts Council of England
- towards the renovation and restoration of our 100 -
year old home. This award has provided us with a
once-in-a-lifetime opportunity to bring our beautiful
and important theatre up to date and redevelopment
work is now in progress at our Sloane Square site.

However we have no wish for change for change's
sake, and the key to our success will be continuity.
The Royal Court's auditorium, for instance, has been
an important factor in the success of the English
Stage Company over 40 years. Nothing must be
done to jeopardise that supportive relationship.
Similarly, the recently improved facade is a much-
loved and familiar face on Sloane Square. This will
scarcely change. But everything else must and will,
not simply because the structure is crumbling and the
mechanical and electrical services outdated. The
Royal Court building must evolve and change to both
maintain its present well-earned position in British
theatre and also to lead the way into the next century.

Building work in Sloane Square is now well underway,
but one major problem remains: the Court must raise
more than £5 million itself in order to complete the
work. The rules of our Lottery award are clear: the
Lottery will pay up to three quarters of the costs of the
capital project but we must find over £5 million
ourselves as Partnership Funding. To help reach our
target, we have launched our *Stage Hands Appeal*
which aims to raise over £500,000 towards this £5
million target from friends, audience members and
the general public by the end of 1998. So far the
appeal has met with great success, but the fact
remains that we still have some way to go to reach our
goal.

If you would like to help, please complete the donation
form enclosed in this playtext (additional donation
forms available from the Box Office) and return it to:
Development Office, Royal Court Theatre Downstairs,
St. Martin's Lane, London WC2N 4BG. For more
information on our redevelment project please call
0171 930 4253. For details on forthcoming productions
in our temporary homes (at the Duke of York's and
Ambassador's Theatres) contact the Box Office on
0171 565 5000.

JERWOOD
NEW PLAYWRIGHTS

The Royal Court is delighted that the relationship with the Jerwood Foundation, which began in 1993, continues in 1997-98 with a third series of *Jerwood New Playwrights*. The Foundation's commitment to supporting new plays by new playwrights has contributed to some of the Court's most successful productions in recent years, including Sebastian Barry's ***The Steward of Christendom***, Mark Ravenhill's ***Shopping and F£££ing*** and Ayub Khan-Din's ***East is East***. This season the

Jerwood New Playwrights series continues to support young theatre with six productions including Conor McPherson's ***The Weir***.

The Jerwood Foundation is a private foundation established in 1977 by the late John Jerwood. It is dedicated to imaginative and responsible funding and sponsorship of the arts, education, design, conservation, medicine, science, engineering and other areas of human endeavour and excellence.

The Beauty Queen of Leenane by Martin McDonagh. Photograph: Ivan Kyncl.

Cockroach Who? by Jess Walters. Photograph: Sean Hudson.

East is East by Ayub Khan-Din. Photograph: Robert Day.

Mojo by Jez Butterworth. Photograph: Ivan Kyncl.

The English Stage Company at the Royal Court Theatre

The English Stage Company was formed to bring serious writing back to the stage. The first Artistic Director, George Devine, wanted to create a vital and popular theatre. He encouraged new writing that explored subjects drawn from contemporary life as well as pursuing European plays and forgotten classics. When John Osborne's **Look Back in Anger** was first produced in 1956, it forced British Theatre into the modern age. In addition to plays by "angry young men", the international repertoire ranged from Brecht to Ionesco, by way of Jean-Paul Sartre, Marguerite Duras, Wedekind and Beckett.

The ambition was to discover new work which was challenging, innovative and also of the highest quality, underpinned by the desire to discover a contemporary style of presentation. Early Court writers included Arnold Wesker, John Arden, David Storey, Ann Jellicoe, N F Simpson and Edward Bond. They were followed by David Hare and Howard Brenton, Caryl Churchill, Timberlake Wertenbaker, Robert Holman and Jim Cartwright. Many of their plays are now regarded as modern classics.

Many established playwrights had their early plays produced in the Theatre Upstairs including Anne Devlin, Andrea Dunbar, Sarah Daniels, Jim Cartwright, Clare McIntyre, Winsome Pinnock, Martin Crimp and Phyllis Nagy. Since 1994 there has been a major season of plays by writers new to the Royal Court, many of them first plays, produced in association with the *Royal National Theatre Studio* with sponsorship from *The Jerwood Foundation*. The writers included Joe Penhall, Nick Grosso, Judy Upton, Sarah Kane, Michael Wynne, Judith Johnson, James Stock, Simon Block and Mark Ravenhill. In 1996-97 The Jerwood Foundation sponsored the Jerwood New Playwrights season, a series of six plays by Jez Butterworth and Martin McDonagh and Ayub Khan-Din (in the Theatre Downstairs), Mark Ravenhill, Tamantha Hammerschlag and Jess Walters (in the Theatre Upstairs).

Theatre Upstairs productions have regularly transferred to the Theatre Downstairs, as with Ariel Dorfman's **Death and the Maiden**, Sebastian Barry's **The Steward of Christendom**, a co-production with *Out of Joint*, and Martin McDonagh's **The Beauty Queen Of Leenane,** a co-production with Druid Theatre Company. Some Theatre Upstairs productions have transferred to the West End, most recently with Kevin Elyot's **My Night With Reg** at the Criterion.

1992-1997 have been record-breaking years at th box-office with capacity houses for productions o **Death and the Maiden, Six Degrees of Separation Oleanna, Hysteria, Cavalcaders, The Kitcher The Queen & I, The Libertine, Simpatico, Moj The Steward of Christendom, The Beauty Quee of Leenane,** and **East is East.**

Death and the Maiden and **Six Degrees o Separation** won the Olivier Award for Best Play i 1992 and 1993 respectively. **Hysteria** won the 199 Olivier Award for Best Comedy, and also the Writers Guild Award for Best West End Play. **My Night wit Reg** won the 1994 Writers' Guild Award for Bes Fringe Play, the Evening Standard Award for Bes Comedy, and the 1994 Olivier Award for Bes Comedy. Jonathan Harvey won the 1994 Evenin Standard Drama Award for Most Promisin Playwright, for **Babies**. Sebastian Barry won th 1995 Writers' Guild Award for Best Fringe Play fo **The Steward of Christendom** and also the 199 Lloyds Private Banking Playwright of the Year Awar Jez Butterworth won the 1995 George Devine Awar for Most Promising Playwright, the 1995 Writers Guild New Writer of the Year, the Evening Standar Award for Most Promising Newcomer and the 199 Olivier Award for Best Comedy for **Mojo**. Phylli Nagy won the 1995 Writers' Guild Award for Bes Regional Play for **Disappeared**. Martin McDonag won the 1996 George Devine Award for Mos Promising Playwright, the 1996 Writers' Guild Bes Fringe Play Award, and the 1996 Evening Standar Drama Award for Most Promising Newcomer fo **The Beauty Queen of Leenane**. The Royal Cou won the 1995 Prudential Award for the Theatre, an was the overall winner of the 1995 Prudential Awar for the Arts for creativity, excellence, innovation an accessibility. The Royal Court won the 1995 Pete Brook Empty Space Award for innovation an excellence in theatre.

Now in its temporary homes, The Duke Of York' and Ambassadors Theatres, during the two-yea refurbishment of its Sloane Square theatre, th Royal Court continues to present the best in ne work. After four decades the company's aims remai consistent with those established by George Devine The Royal Court is still a major focus in the countr for the production of new work. Scores of plays firs seen at the Royal Court are now part of the nationa and international dramatic repertoire.

THE WEIR

by Conor McPherson

Cast

Jim Kieran Ahern
Brendan Brendan Coyle
Valerie Julia Ford
Finbar Gerard Horan
Jack Jim Norton

Director Ian Rickson
Designer Rae Smith
Lighting Designer Paule Constable
Sound Designer Paul Arditti
Music Stephen Warbeck
Assistant Director Annabelle Comyn
Production Manager Paul Handley
Company Stage Manger Maris Sharp
Stage Managers Katy Hastings
Lisa Buckley
Costume Supervisor Jennifer Cook
Production Photographs Pau Ros

The Ambassadors Theatre was re-designed by William Dudley.

 he Royal Court would like to thank the following with this production:Wardrobe care by Persil and Comfort
urtesy of Lever Brothers Ltd, refrigerators by Electrolux and Philips Major Appliances Ltd.; kettles for
hearsals by Morphy Richards; video for casting purposes by Hitachi; backstage coffee machine by West 9;
rniture by Knoll International; freezer for backstage use supplied by Zanussi Ltd 'Now that's a good idea.' Hair
yling by Carole at Moreno, 2 Holbein Place, Sloane Square 0171- 730- 0211; Closed circuit TV cameras and
onitors by Mitsubishi UK Ltd. Natural spring water from Aqua Cool, 12 Waterside Way, London SW17 0XH, tel.
81-947 5666. Overhead projector from W.H. Smith; Sanyo U.K for the backstage microwave; Mr Tom Perrott,
hairman of the Ghost Club of Great Britain; Professor Arthur Ellison, President of Society for Psychical
esearch; Ms A S Sumitri-Mills, Chartered Counselling Psychologist of the Charter of Medical England Ltd; John
ddle of Hogshead Breweries; Charlotte Gwinner; The Roundhouse; Photo re-touching and restoration
onsored by Snappy Snaps 0181 741 7474; Weir picture from Environment Agency; KP Foods; Linden Goode
Auto Bar; Bord Failte; North West Tourism Authority, Sligo; Guinness Brewery; Micheal Coughlan at Rí-Rá
agazine; Opie's the Stove Shop.

Conor McPherson (writer)
Theatre includes: The Stars Lose Their Glory, A Light in the Window of Industry, Radio Play, Rum and Vodka, The Good Thief - Winner of the 1995 Stewart Parker Award (Fly By Night Theatre Company, Dublin); This Lime Tree Bower (Bush / Winner Guinness Ingenuity Award, Meyer Whitworth Award, and won him a Pearson Television Theatre Writer's Residency Award for 1996); St Nicholas (Bush).
Radio: This Lime Tree Bower (to be broadcast in August).
Film includes: I Went Down (Treasure Films, BBC Films).

Kieran Ahern
For the Royal Court: The Steward of Christendom (and Out of Joint).
Other theatre includes: School for Wives, Volpone, The Overcoat, Normal (Meridian); The Illusion (Charabanc); Tartuffe (The Gate, Dublin); Moll (Cork Opera House); The Government Inspector (Everyman); The Broken Kiss (Andrews Lane); Lady Windermere's Fan (Rough Magic); The Odd Couple, Bedroom Farce (Playwrights & Actors).
TV includes: Tough Love, Great Love Stories, Against the Wind, Edward No Hands, The Matchmaker, The Governor, Before I Sleep.

Paul Arditti (sound designer)
Paul has been a Sound Designer since 1983. By 1985 he was a member of the National Theatre's sound department, where he stayed until 1988, designing extensively for Sir Peter Hall. Paul worked freelance until 1993, when he became involved with the Royal Court Theatre under Stephen Daldry. Since then, Paul has enjoyed a dual career as Head of Sound at the Court, and as a freelance Sound Designer. Paul was awarded the Drama Desk Award for Outstanding Sound Design in 1992.
Sound Designs this year include:
For the Royal Court: Attempts on Her Life, Shopping and F£££ing (& Gielgud).
Other theatre: The Merry Wives of Windsor, Hamlet (RSC); The Illusion (Royal Exchange, Manchester).

Paule Constable (lighting designer)
Theatre includes: The Mysteries (RSC); The Caucasian Chalk Circle (RNT); Henry IV Parts 1 & 2 (English Touring Theatre); Poor Super Man (Manchester Royal Exchange).
Opera includes: productions for the English National, Welsh and Scottish Operas; Garsington Opera Festival; Guildhall School; Bright Young Things (Birmingham Royal Ballet at the Royal Opera House).

In preparation: Sweeney Todd (Opera North); Fidel (New Zealand International Festival of the Arts Macbeth (Bristol Old Vic & Tour); season of Becke plays (RSC).

Brendan Coyle
For the Royal Court: The Changing Room (Roy Court Classics, Duke of York's), Pygmies in the Ruin Other theatre includes: Playboy of the Western Worl Over the Bridge, All Souls Night (Lyric, Belfast); Th Ragged Trousered Philanthropists (UK tour); Th Plough and the Stars (UK and Eire tours); Elegie (King's Head and Drill Hall); Judgement Day (Old Re Lion); September Tide (King's Head and Comedy Philadelphia Here I Come (King's Head ar Wyndham's) The Love Song for Ulster Trilog (Tricycle); The Silver Tassie (Almeida); Force ar Hypocrisy (Young Vic).
Television includes: The Glass Virgin, Dangerfiel The Full Wax, The Bill, London Calling, Silent Witnes Thieftakers.
Film includes: Ailsa, London Calling, The Cull, Th Last Bus Home, Tomorrow Never Dies.

Julia Ford
For the Royal Court: The Shallow End, Some Singir Blood.
Other theatre includes: Now You Know (Hampstead The Lodger (Royal Exchange and Hampstead Chinese Wolf (Bush Theatre); Hamlet (Riversid Studios and tour); A Doll's House, Who's Afraid Virginia Woolf? (Wolsey Theatre, Ipswich); Pool Bethesda (Orange Tree); Piano, The Crucible, Yerm School for Wives (RNT); The Blood of Others (RN Studio); Jumping the Rug (RSC/Almeida Festival The Duchess of Malfi, Two Wheel Tricycle, The Mothe A Midsummer Night's Dream (Contact Theatr Manchester); Knickers (Bristol Old Vic); Th Plantagenets, King John, Much Ado About Nothin (RSC); Venus and Adonis (Almeida); Accrington Pal Tartuffe, The Railway Children, Touched (Oldha Coliseum).
Television includes: Insiders, Accused, Eight Hou from Paris, The Bill, Strike Force, Medics, Blood an Fire, Peak Practice, The Healer, In Suspiciou Circumstances, A Skirt Through History, Casualty, Fatal Inversion, Bergerac,The Continental, The Ritz The Practice.

Gerard Horan
For the Royal Court: Up to the Sun, Built on San Downfall, Saved, The Pope's Wedding, A Whistle the Dark, Rat in the Skull.
Other theatre includes: Rat in the Skull (Public Theatre New York); Man and Superman (Citizens, Glasgow Public Enemy, Look Back in Anger, A Midsummer

ght's Dream, King Lear, Coriolanus (Renaissance Theatre); The Plough and the Stars (West Yorkshire Playhouse); Sod (Edinburgh Festival); Blue Remembered Hills (RNT).

Television includes: The Singing Detective, London's Burning, Les Girls, Palmer, The Grass Arena, Shoot to Kill, Look Back in Anger, Life After Life, Soldier Soldier, Cruel Train, The Icehouse, Snap!

Film includes: My Beautiful Launderette, Sammy and Rosie Get Laid, Hidden City, Chicago Joe and the Showgirl, Much Ado About Nothing, Frankenstein, Immortal Beloved, In the Bleak Midwinter, Crossing the Border, Les Miserables.

im Norton

For the Royal Court: The Contractor (& Fortune), The Changing Room (& Globe).

Other theatre includes: A Chorus of Disapproval (RNT & Lyric); Bedroom Farce (Prince of Wales); The Comedians (RNT & Wyndhams); Way Upstream, Playboy of the Western World, Mandragola, St Joan, Tamburlaine the Great, Hamlet, Emigres (RNT); The Wild Duck (Lyric, Hammersmith); A Kind of Alaska, The Bread Man, Bloomsday (Gate, Dublin); Juno and the Paycock (Gaiety); Drums of Father Ned, Entertaining Mr Sloane (Olympia, Dublin); Red Roses for Me, Tarry Flynn, Boss Grady's Boys (Abbey); White Woman Street (Bush & Abbey); Zoo Story (Eblana, Dublin); She Stoops to Folly (South Coast Repertory Los Angeles & Abbey); Someone Who'll Watch Over Me (South Coast Repertory Los Angeles).

Television includes: The Ambassador, Father Ted, Lovejoy, Maigret, Poirot, The Temptation of Eileen Hughes, Ike and Monty, Great Writers, Mr Palfrey of Westminster, Rumpole of the Bailey, Reith, Tales of the Unexpected, Nanny, Minder, Juno and the Paycock, Two's Company, Againstthe Wind, People Like Us, Van Der Valk, Black Beauty, Sam, The Sweeney, Fall of the Eagles, Colditz, Death of Captain Doughty, Cruel Doubt, Star Trek: The Next Generation, Babylon Five, Cheers, LA Law, Frazier.

Film includes: Hidden Agenda, Into the West, Memoires of an Invisible Man, Sakharov, Mr Joyce is Leaving Paris, Straw Dogs.

Ian Rickson (director)

For the Royal Court: The Lights, Pale Horse, Mojo (& Steppenwolf Theatre Co., Chicago), Ashes and Sand, Some Voices, Killers (1992 Young Writers' Festival), Wildfire.

Other theatre includes: The House of Yes (Gate Theatre); Me and My Friend (Chichester Festival Theatre); Queer Fish (BAC); First Strike (Soho Poly); Minty (Irish tour).

Opera includes: La Serva Padrona (Broomhill).

Ian is an Associate Director at the Royal Court.

Rae Smith (designer)

For the Royal Court: Some Voices.

Theatre includes: Boundaries for Men (Roof of the South Bank); Sarrasine, Mrs Warren's Profession, A Christmas Carol, The Letter (Lyric, Hammersmith); Endgame (Donmar Warehouse); Silence Silence Silence (Mladinsko Theatre); The Phoenician Women, Henry IV (RSC); The Mosquitto Coast, Gormenghast (David Glass Ensemble); Charley's Aunt (Manchester Royal Exchange); A Midsummer Night's Dream (Royal Lyceum, Edinburgh); Death of a Salesman (West Yorkshire Playhouse); The Europeans (Wrestling School); Designs for Theatre de Complicite - The Visit (Time Out Award), Help I'm Alive, Ave Maria, Wiseguy Scapino, The Street of Crocodiles.

As director & designer: Lucky (David Glass Ensemble); Mysteria (RSC); Terminator (Royal National Studio). Designs for opera include: Don Giovanni (Welsh National Opera); The Magic Flute (Opera North); Shameless (Opera Circus).

She has received two design awards for working sabbaticals in Indonesia and Japan.

Current projects: The Cocktail Party (Royal Lyceum, Edinburgh); The Arbour (RNT Studio); Cause Celebre (Lyric, Hammersmith).

Stephen Warbeck (music)

For the Royal Court: Harry and Me, Simpatico, The Editing Process, Some Voices, The Kitchen, Blood, A Lie of the Mind, Greenland, Bloody Poetry, Built on Sand, Royal Borough, Downfall.

Other theatre music includes: An Inspector Calls (transferred to Broadway & Tokyo), Machinal, At Our Table, The Mother, Roots, Magic Olympical Games (RNT); The Taming of the Shrew, The Cherry Orchard, The White Devil, Cymbeline (RSC); Damned for Despair, Figaro Gets Divorced, Pioneers & Purgatory in Ingolstadt, Canterbury Tales, Judgement Day (Gate Theatre).

Recent TV music includes: Prime Suspect (BAFTA nomination); The Changeling, Skallagrigg (BAFTA nomination); You Me and Marley; Bitter Harvest; In the Border Country; Roots; Nona; Happy Feet; Bambino Mio; Meat; Blood & Water; Devil's Advocate; Bramwell; The Chemistry Lesson, Nervous Energy, Truth or Dare.

Film scores include: Sister My Sister; O Mary This London; Marooned; Crossing the Border, Mrs Brown, My Son the Fanatic.

Stephen has also written music for many BBC Radio plays, writes for his band The hKippers, and the Metropolitan Water Board.

For the Royal Court

DIRECTION
Artistic Director
Stephen Daldry
Assistant to the Artistic Director
Marieke Spencer
Deputy Director
James Macdonald
Associate Directors
Elyse Dodgson
Ian Rickson
Garry Hynes*
Max Stafford-Clark*
Caroline Hall*
Roxana Silbert*
Stephen Warbeck *(music)*
Trainee Director
Rufus Norris #
Casting Director
Lisa Makin
Literary Manager
Graham Whybrow
Literary Assistant
Jean O'Hare
Literary Associate
Stephen Jeffreys*
Resident Dramatist
Martin Crimp+
International Assistant
Aurélie Mérel
Artistic Assistant
Rachael Prior

PRODUCTION
Production Manager
Edwyn Wilson
Deputy Production Manager
Paul Handley
Production Development Manager
Simon Harper
Head of Lighting
Johanna Town
Senior Electricians
Alison Buchanan
Lizz Poulter
Assistant Electricians
Marion Mahon
Lars Jensen
LX Board Operator
Michelle Green
Head of Stage
Martin Riley
Senior Carpenters
David Skelly
Christopher Shepherd
Terry Bennett
Head of Sound
Paul Arditti
Deputy Sound
Simon King
Sound Assistant
Neil Alexander
Production Assistant
Mark Townsend
Head of Wardrobe
Jennifer Cook
Costume Deputies
Neil Gillies
Heather Tomlinson

MANAGEMENT
Executive Director
Vikki Heywood
Assistant to the Executive Director
Diana Pao
Administrator
Alpha Hopkins
Finance Director
Donna Munday
Finance Officer
Rachel Harrison
Re-development Finance Officer
Neville Ayres
Project Manager
Tony Hudson
Assistant to Project Manager
Monica McCormack
Finance & Administration Assistant
Sarah Deacon

MARKETING & PRESS
Marketing Manager
Jess Cleverly
Press Manager
(0171-565 5055)
Anne Mayer
Marketing Co-ordinator
Lisa Popham
Publicity Assistant
Peter Collins
Box Office Manager
Neil Grutchfield
Deputy Box Office Manager
Terry Cooke
Box Office Sales Operators
Glen Bowman
Valli Dakshinamurthi
Ian Golding
Emma O'Neill
Ruth Goucheron*
Azieb Zerai*

DEVELOPMENT
Development Director
Caroline Underwood
Head of Development
Joyce Hytner*
Development Manager
Jacqueline Simons
Development Co-ordinator
Susie Songhurst*
Development Assistant
Tracey Nowell

FRONT OF HOUSE
Theatre Manager
Gary Stewart
Deputy Theatre Managers
Yvette Griffith
Tim Brunsden
Duty House Manager
Rachel Fisher*
Relief Duty House Managers
Sarah Harrison*
Anthony Corriette*
Lorraine Selby*
Jemma Davies*
Bookshop Supervisors
Del Campbell*

Maintenance
Greg Piggot*
Lunch Bar Caterer
Andrew Forrest*
Stage Door/Reception
Jemma Davies*
Lorraine Benloss*
Charlotte Frings*
Tyrone Lucas*
Andonis Anthony*
Tom Cockrell*
Cleaners
(Theatre Upstairs)
Maria Correia*
Mila Hamovic*
Peter Ramswell*
(Theatre Downstairs)
Avery Cleaning Services Ltd.
Fireman
Myriad Security Services
(Theatre Downstairs)
Datem Fire Safety Services
(Theatre Upstairs)

YOUNG PEOPLE'S THEATRE
Director
Carl Miller
Youth Drama Worker
Ollie Animashawun
Special Projects
Julie-Anne Robinson
Administrator
Aoife Mannix
Outreach Co-ordinator
Stephen Gilroy

Thanks to all of our
bar staff and ushers

*=part-time
#=Arts Council of England/Calouste Gulbenkian Foundation/Esmeé Fairbairn Charitable Trust
+ = Arts Council Resident Dramatist

THE WEIR

For Michael, Clare, Karen and Margaret
And for Gina

Author's Note

There are some differences in this text compared to the show you
will see at the Royal Court. Here is an example why this happens.

The play has already been published along with *St Nicholas*, and so
the publishers had what they considered a clean version, ready to
go, to coincide with this production. However, this production
couldn't accommodate some of the ideas in the original play. For
instance, it was felt that drinking something that looks like draught
Guinness on stage was impossible because the only thing that looks
like draught stout *is* draught stout. And it was decided that it was
unfair to the actors to have to drink alcohol on stage. (Although in
reality they're probably quite disappointed.)

The original version begins with Jack pouring himself a pint of
stout in Brendan's bar. I had to rewrite. We could've had him pour
a pint of non-alcoholic lager, pretending it's real lager, but
something in me can't conceive of him drinking anything but stout.
So I decided to have him drink bottles because the Guinness tap is
broken. He'd only have to drink half the amount. But now we run
into further problems. I had to go through the whole play changing
the drinks, and have Jack explain to newcomers why he's drinking
bottles as opposed to pints, a fact that simply would not go
unremarked in the type of place where the play is set. So the whole
beginning of the play is different.

There are other changes due to practical constraints but that's the
biggest one and it's a good example of how these things happen.

I hope you like ghost stories.

Characters

JACK, *fifties.*
BRENDAN, *thirties.*
JIM, *forties.*
FINBAR, *late forties.*
VALERIE, *thirties.*

The play is set in a rural part of Ireland, Northwest Leitrim or Sligo. Present day. Stage Setting: a small rural bar.

A counter; left with three bar taps. The spirits are not mounted, simply left on the shelf. There are three stools at the counter.

There is a fireplace, right. Near this is a low table with some small stools and a bigger, more comfortable chair, nearest the fire. There is another small table, front, with a stool or two.

On the wall, back, are some old black and white photographs, A ruined Abbey. People posing near a newly erected ESB weir. A town in a cove with mountains around it.

An old television is mounted up in a corner, right. There is a small radio on a shelf behind the bar.

A door, right, is the main entrance to the bar. A door, back, leads to the toilets and a yard.

This bar is part of a house and the house is part of a farm.

The door, right, opens. JACK comes in. He wears a suit which looks a bit big for him, and a white shirt open at the collar. Over this is a dirty anorak. He takes the anorak off and hangs it up. He wipes his boots aggressively on a mat.

He goes behind the counter. He selects a glass and pours himself a pint of stout. He puts it on the bar and turns to the till, which he opens with practised, if uncertain, ease. He puts the money in and takes the change.

As he does this, the door at back opens. BRENDAN comes in. He wears a sweater, heavy cord pants and a pair of slip-on shoes. He carries a bucket with peat briquettes. He goes to the fire, barely acknowledging JACK, just his voice.

BRENDAN. Jack.

JACK. Brendan.

BRENDAN (*tending the fire*). That's some wind.

JACK (*topping up his pint*). It is.

BRENDAN. Must have been against you, was it?

> JACK *comes out from behind the counter and stands looking at the fire.*

JACK. It was. It was against me till I came around the Knock. It was a bit of shelter then.

1

BRENDAN *also stands looking at the fire.*

BRENDAN. Yeah it's a funny one. It's coming from the north.

JACK. Mm. Ah, it's mild enough though.

BRENDAN. Ah yeah. It's balmy enough. (*Pause.*) It's balmy enough.

BRENDAN *goes in behind the counter.*

JACK. Were you in Carrick today?

BRENDAN. I wasn't, no. I had the sisters over doing their rounds. Checking up on me.

JACK. Checking their investments.

BRENDAN. Oh yeah. Course, they don't have a fucking clue what they're looking for, d'you know? They're just vaguely . . . you know.

JACK. Keeping the pressure on you.

BRENDAN. This is it. (*Pause.*) At me to sell the top field.

JACK. You don't use it much.

BRENDAN. No. No I don't. Too much trouble. Driving a herd up. But I know they're looking at it, all they see is new cars for their hubbies, you know?

JACK. Mm. You're not just trying to spite them? Get them vexed? Hah?

BRENDAN. Not at all. I'm, just. It's a grand spot up there. Ah, I don't know. Just . . . (*Short pause.*)

JACK. They over the whole day?

BRENDAN. They got here about two. They'd gone for lunch in the Arms. Got their story straight. Ah they were gone and all about half four.

JACK. They've no attachment to the place, no?

BRENDAN. No they don't. They look around, and it's . . . 'Ah yeah . . . ' you know? (*They laugh a little.*)

BRENDAN. It's gas.

JACK. Mm.

BRENDAN. Were you in Carrick yourself?

JACK. I was. I flew in about eleven, threw on a fast bet. Jimmy was there, we went for a quick one in the Pot.

BRENDAN. How's Jimmy? And the ma?

2

JACK. Ah. Jimmy. Be in tonight. He put me on to a nice one. We got her at eleven to four.

BRENDAN. You're learning to listen, hah?

JACK. Ah. Fuck that sure. I know, but I've been having the worst run of shit, you wouldn't believe. I was that desperate, I'd listen to anybody.

BRENDAN. Go on out of that.

JACK. Ah no. No no. Fair dues. I'll say it. He got us a right one. And it's good, you know. Break a streak like that.

BRENDAN. You're a user.

JACK (*laughs*). There's worse.

BRENDAN. Yeah. There might be.

JACK. But, ah, he was telling me. Did you know about Maura Nealon's house?

BRENDAN. No.

JACK. Well. Jim says he met Finbar Mack down in the Spar. Finally, either sold or's renting the, the thing, after how many years it's sat there?

BRENDAN. Jays, four or five in anyway.

JACK. Jim says five this month. And Finbar's going bananas with the great fella that he is. Patting himself on the back, goodo, and talking about the new resident. Who, he says, is a fine girl. Single. Down from Dublin and all this. And Finbar's nearly leaving the wife just to have a chance with this one. Only messing, like. But he's going to bring her in here tonight. This is the nearest place to old Maura's. Bring her in for a drink, introduce her to the natives.

BRENDAN. The dirty bastard. I don't want him using in here for that sort of carry on. A married man like him.

JACK. Ah he's only old shit. He wouldn't have the nerve. Sure, how far'd he get anyway? The fucking head on him. He's only having a little thrill. Bringing her around. And I'll tell you what it is as well. He's coming in here with her. And he's the one. He's the one that's 'with' her, in whatever fucking . . . sense we're talking about. He's bringing her in. And there's you and me, and the Jimmy fella, the muggins's, the single fellas. And he's the married fella. And he's going 'Look at this! There's obviously something the fuck wrong with yous. Yous are single and you couldn't get a woman near this place. And look at me. I'm hitched. I'm over and done with, and I'm having to beat them off.'

BRENDAN. Yeah. That's the way cunts always go about their business. It's intrusive, it's bad manners, it's . . .

JACK. Ah, it's a juvenile carry on. You know?

BRENDAN. Mm.

JACK. Let her come in herself.

BRENDAN. Yeah. That'd be better. That'd make more sense, for fuck's sake.

JACK. Leave her be . . . (*Short pause.*) Don't know if I'll stay actually.

BRENDAN. Mm.

Pause. JACK *drains his pint and brings his glass to the bar.*

JACK. Go on.

BRENDAN *takes the glass and pours a fresh pint.*

JACK. Don't want to leave Jimmy in the lurch. You know? Trying to hold his own in the Finbar Mack world of big business.

They laugh a little.

BRENDAN. Fucking . . . Jimmy talking all that crack with Finbar.

JACK. But that's the thing though. The Jimmy fella's got more going on up here (*Head.*) than popular opinion would give him credit for.

BRENDAN. Sure, don't we know too well, for God's sake?

JACK. I know.

BRENDAN. We know only too well.

JACK *counts change out on the bar.*

JACK. Would you give us ten Silk Cut please, Brendan?

BRENDAN. Red?

JACK. Please.

BRENDAN *hands over the cigarettes and finishes pulling the pint.*

JACK. Good man.

BRENDAN *counts the money off the bar.* JACK *pauses before drinking.*

JACK. Are we right?

BRENDAN. Close enough. Cheers.

JACK. Good luck.

JACK *takes a long drink. Pause.*

JACK. I know I do be at you. I'll keep at you though.

BRENDAN. About what?

JACK. Don't be messing. Come on.

BRENDAN. Ah.

JACK. A young fella like you. And this place a right going concern.

BRENDAN. Ah. The odd time. You know, the odd time I'd think about it.

JACK. You should though.

BRENDAN. Well then, so should you.

JACK. Would you go on? An auld fella like me!

BRENDAN. Would you listen to him?

JACK. Ah, sure what would I want with giving up my freedom?

BRENDAN. Well then me as well!

Pause.

JACK. Tch. Maybe. Maybe there's something to be said for the old independence.

BRENDAN. Ah there is.

Pause.

JACK. A lot to be said for it.

BRENDAN. Mm. (*Pause.*) Mm.

JACK. Cheers!

BRENDAN. Good luck.

JACK *takes a long drink. The main door opens and* JIMMY *enters. He takes off an anorak to reveal a festive looking cardigan.* JACK *pretends not to notice him.*

JACK (*winks*). Oh yes, Brendan, the luck is changing. I got me and the Jimmy fella onto a nice one today. That fella would want to listen to me a little more often, I tell you.

JIM. I'm going to have to start charging you for tips, am I?

JACK. Ah James! What'll you have?

JIM. Teach you some manners. Teach him some manners Brendan, ha? Small one please Jack.

BRENDAN. Small one.

JACK. Sure it'd take more than money to put manners on me, ha? Brendan.

5

BRENDAN. It'd take a bomb under you.

JACK. Now you said it. Bomb is right. That wind still up, Jim?

JIM. Oh it is, yeah. Warm enough though.

JACK. We were just saying.

BRENDAN. For a Northerly.

JIM. Oh that's from the west now.

BRENDAN. Is it?

JIM. Oh yeah that's a Westerly.

JACK. Must've shifted.

JIM. Mm.

> *Pause.* JIM *comes to the bar.*

JIM. Thanking you.

JACK. Good luck.

JIM. Good luck.

BRENDAN. Good luck.

> JACK *counts change out on the bar.*

JACK. Are we right?

> BRENDAN *counts and pushes a coin back towards* JACK.

BRENDAN (*taking rest*). Now we are. Sure it's hard enough to come by without giving it away.

JACK. This is it. Oh. (*To* JIM.) Are you doing anything tomorrow?

JIM. What time?

JACK. I have to get out to Conor Boland. His tractor is packed up. And I have Father Donal's jalopy in since Tuesday. Said I'd change the oil. Haven't done it yet. Would you come in and do it so I can go over to Boland's?

JIM. It'd have to be early. I'm dropping the mother out to Sligo.

JACK. Well, whatever. Is that all right?

JIM. Ah, it should be yeah. Pint?

JACK. Not for the moment. You go on.

JIM. Pint please Brendan.

BRENDAN. How's the mammy today?

JIM. Ah you know?

JACK. Tch. I have to get down and see her. I keep saying it.

6

JIM. Well whenever, whenever you want.

BRENDAN. Do you think you'll do anything?

JIM. About?

BRENDAN. About up there on your own and all that?

JIM. Ah. Sure where would I go? And I was talking to Finbar
Mack. Be lucky to get twenty thousand for the place. Sure where
would you be going with that? (*Short pause.*) You know!

JACK. With the acre?

JIM. Ah yeah, the whole . . . the whole thing.

JACK. Ah you're grand with the few little jobs around here.

JIM. Ah.

JACK. You'll be cosy enough.

Pause.

BRENDAN. Jack was telling me about Finbar. And the new eh . . .

JIM. Mmm, yeah, I was telling him earlier.

JACK. I was telling him.

JIM. I've seen her since.

BRENDAN. Oh yeah?

JIM. Yeah, they were in Finbar's car going up the Head.

JACK *and* BRENDAN *exchange a look.*

BRENDAN. Fucking hell.

JACK. Like a courting couple or something.

JIM. He's showing her the area.

JACK. Jesus. 'The area.' He's a terrible fucking thick.

JIM. Ah, he has them all jabbering down in Carrick.

JACK. Yeah. I wish he wasn't bringing her in here. You know?

BRENDAN. Sure he hasn't been in here since Freddie Mack
drowned.

JACK. What the fuck, is he doing? You know?

JIM. Ah. She's new. This is the only place near to her.

JACK. She can . . . (*Nodding.*) find her own way surely, Jim,
come on.

BRENDAN. Well it's, you know. If it's courtesy, which is one
thing and a business . . . act or whatever, you know, you have to
say, well . . . you know, okay. But if it's all messy, I'm trapped

in here behind this fucking thing. And you wish he'd stop acting the mess. I have to respect whatever, they're . . .

JACK. Well this is it, we're here.

JIM. It's probably not really anything.

Short pause.

JACK. What age would she be, about, Jim?

JIM. Em, I only saw her for a sec. I'd say, (*Beat.*) like they were in the car and all, I'd say about thirties. Very nice looking.

Pause.

JACK. Dublin woman.

JIM. Dublin.

Short pause.

BRENDAN. She's no one in the area, no?

JIM. No she's . . . coming down, you know?

JACK. Mm. (*Pause.*) Yeah.

JIM. Good luck. (*Drinks.*)

JACK. Cheers. (*Drinks.*)

BRENDAN. Good luck, boys.

JACK. Another week or two now, You'll be seeing the first of the Germans.

BRENDAN. Mm. Stretch in the evening, yeah.

JACK. You wouldn't ever think of clearing one of the fields for a few caravans.

BRENDAN. Ah.

JACK. The top field.

BRENDAN. Ah there wouldn't be a lot of shelter up there. There'd be a wind up there that'd cut you.

JIM. D'you know what you could do? The herd'd be grand up there, and you could, you know, down here.

BRENDAN. Ah. (*Short pause.*) They do be around anyway. You know yourself.

JIM. Ah, they do.

JACK. You're not chasing the extra revenue.

BRENDAN. Or the work!

JIM. They do be around right enough.

BRENDAN. I'll leave the campsites to Finbar, ha? He'll sort them out.

JACK. Ah, Finbar's in need of the few shekels.

They laugh.

BRENDAN. Ah, he's in dire need of the few bob, the poor fella, that's right, that's right.

JACK. Mm.

Pause.

BRENDAN. Yeah. If you had all the . . . families out there. On their holliers. And all the kids and all. You'd feel the evenings turning. When they'd be leaving. And whatever about how quiet it is now. It'd be fucking shocking quiet then. (*Short pause.*) You know?

Pause.

JACK. Mm.

JIM. D'you want a small one, Jack?

JACK. Go on.

JIM. Two small ones please Brendan.

BRENDAN. The small fellas.

BRENDAN *works.*

JACK. Are you having one yourself?

BRENDAN. I'm debating whether to have one.

JACK. Ah have one, and don't be acting the mess.

BRENDAN. Go on then.

He pours himself a glass of whiskey.

JACK. Good man. (*Short pause.*) A few shekels, ha? (*They smile.*) Mm.

JACK *takes out his cigarettes.*

JACK. Jim?

JIM. Oh cheers Jack.

JIM *takes one.*

JACK. Brendan?

BRENDAN. Fags and all, ha?

JACK. Go on, they're good for you.

BRENDAN. (*Taking one.*) Go on.

They light up from a match which JACK *strikes. They puff contentedly for a moment.*

JIM (*lifting glass*). Keep the chill out.

JACK. This is it. Cheers.

BRENDAN. Cheers men.

JIM. Good luck.

They drink.

JACK. Now.

JIM. D'yous hear a car?

Pause.

BRENDAN. No.

JIM. That's Finbar's car.

Pause.

JIM. He's parked.

JACK. I didn't see the lights.

JIM. He came around the Knock.

From off, they hear FINBAR's *voice.*

FINBAR (*off*). Ah yeah, sure half the townland used to nearly live in here.

JACK. There we are now.

The door opens and FINBAR *brings* VALERIE *in.*

FINBAR. That's it now.

FINBAR *wears a light cream coloured suit and an open collar.* VALERIE *wears jeans and a sweater.*

FINBAR. Men. This is Valerie. She's just moved into Maura Nealon's old house.

JACK. Hello, how are you?

JACK *shakes her hand.*

VALERIE. Hello.

FINBAR. This is Jack Mullen. He has a little garage up around the Knock.

VALERIE. How are you?

JACK *nods politely.*

JACK. Now.

FINBAR. This is Jim Curran. Does a bit of work with Jack.

10

VALERIE *and* JIM *shake hands.*

VALERIE. Pleased to meet you.

JIM. Pleased to meet you.

FINBAR. And this is Brendan. Brendan Byrne.

VALERIE. Hello.

They shake hands.

BRENDAN. How are you?

FINBAR. This is his bar. And all the land I showed you. All back down the hill. That's all his farm.

VALERIE. Oh right. It's all lovely here.

BRENDAN. Oh yeah. It's a grand spot all along . . . for going for a walk or that, all down the cliffs.

FINBAR. Oh it's lovely all down here. What'll you have?

BRENDAN. Oh, I'll get this, Finbar. No. What, what do you want?

FINBAR. Oh now, ha ha. Eh, I'll have a pint, then, what? Says you, if it's going, ha?

BRENDAN. Pint. Valerie?

VALERIE. Em. Could I have . . . Do you have . . . em, a glass of white wine?

Pause.

BRENDAN (*going*). Yeah. I'm just going to run in the house.

VALERIE Oh no. Don't. Don't put yourself to any trouble.

BRENDAN. No. No it's no trouble. I have a bottle.

He goes.

FINBAR. He probably has a bottle of the old vino, from feckin . . . Christmas, what?

JACK. It's not too often the . . . the . . . wine does be flowing in here.

VALERIE. I'm all embarrassed now.

FINBAR. Don't be silly. Sit up there now, and don't mind us. Don't mind these country fellas.

JACK. Jays. You're not long out of it yourself, says the man, ha?

FINBAR (*winks*). They're only jealous Valerie because I went to the town to seek my fortune. And they all stayed out here on the bog picking their holes.

JACK. Janey, now ha? You didn't have very hard to seek. Just a quick look in big Finbar's will, I think is more like it.

FINBAR. Big Finbar's will! That's shrewd investment, boy. That's an eye for the gap.

JACK. Yeah, he probably fleeced you on Maura Nealon's house, did he?

VALERIE. I have to say I don't think so.

FINBAR. Good girl.

VALERIE. But it's very reasonable all around here, isn't it?

FINBAR. Oh it is, yeah . You know . . .

Short pause.

JACK. Is there much doing up in it?

FINBAR. Ah, hardly any.

VALERIE. There's one or two floorboards. A bit of paint.

JACK (*indicating* JIM). Well, there's your man. If you're looking for a good pair of hands.

VALERIE. Is that right?

JIM. I'll have a look for you, if you like. I know that house.

FINBAR Don't be charging her through the nose now.

JIM. Ah ha, now.

BRENDAN *returns with a bottle of wine.*

FINBAR. You'd want to be giving her a neighbourly . . . rate, now, is the thing, ha?

JIM. Oh yeah.

JACK. Would you listen to him? 'Neighbourly rates'. Wasn't by giving neighbourly rates you bought half the fucking town.

FINBAR. Half the town! (*To* VALERIE, *winking.*) I bought the whole town. Eye for the gap, you see.

JACK. Eye for your gap is right.

FINBAR (*To* BRENDAN). How long has that been in there? Lying in some drawer . . .

BRENDAN (*corkscrewing the bottle*). Ah, it was a . . . present or some . . . (*Looks at label.*) 1990. Now. Vintage, ha? (*They laugh.*) I hope it's all right now.

VALERIE. It's grand. I won't know the difference.

They watch BRENDAN *open the bottle. He pours a tumbler full and holds it up to the light and sniffs it.*

BRENDAN. I think it's all right.

FINBAR. Ah, would you give the woman the feckin thing. The tongue's hanging out of her.

Again they watch as VALERIE *takes the glass.*

VALERIE. Thanks Brendan.

She drinks.

VALERIE. That's gorgeous. I'm not joking now. That's lovely.

FINBAR. Good.

BRENDAN. I'm putting it in the fridge for you Valerie.

He does.

FINBAR. Good man.

Pause. FINBAR *nods at* VALERIE, *a reassuring 'hello'.*

(*To* JACK *and* JIM.) How d'yous do today, boys?

JACK. Are you codding me? With this fella? Eleven to four we got her at, came down to six to four.

FINBAR. Sheer Delight was it?

JACK. Yeah. Kenny down in the shop, the knacker. Adjusting everything how this fella's betting.

JIM (*indicating* JACK). This fella hardly listens to me.

JACK. Ah now.

FINBAR. He's too proud, Jimmy. Too proud to admit when he needs a tip off you.

JACK (*emphatically*). I . . . have . . . my policy on this. And I have my principle. I am the first one to say it about this fella. See, usually, Valerie, usually, not all the time, Jim's not too far off the mark.

FINBAR. 'Too far off the mark!' (*To* VALERIE.) He's bang on the nail!

BRENDAN *places a pint on the bar.*

FINBAR. Thanks Brendan.

He puts his hand in his pocket, BRENDAN *waves him away.*

JACK. Not every time.

FINBAR. Thanks, thanks a million. (*To* VALERIE.) He is.

JACK. Bang on the nail is one thing, from judgement . . . and . . . But, and Jimmy knows I don't mean anything by this, and I know because we've spoken about this before. He has a scientific approach. He studies the form. And, no offence, he has a bit of time to be doing that. He studies it Valerie, and fair play to him, right? Do you bet on horses?

VALERIE. No.

FINBAR. Good girl.

JACK. Well he, how much, Jim, would you make in a month? On the horses.

JIM. Ah it evens out Jack. Like I'm not eh . . . I don't . . .

JACK. How much was it you got that time? When Cheltenham was on that time.

JIM. Two hundred and twenty.

JACK. Two hundred and twenty pounds, Valerie, in like three days, now. Right?

JIM. Yeah but . . .

JACK. Yeah, I know, that'd be a bigger win. But he was planning for Cheltenham for weeks, Valerie, and . . . tinkering with his figures and his . . . you know. He'd be in here with the paper up on the counter there. Brendan? Before Cheltenham?

BRENDAN. Oh yeah.

JACK. Right? Now, but I'm more: 'Ah, sure, I'll have an old bet, like.' Do you know that way? And that's what I do, and to tell you the truth I don't be too bothered. It's a bit of fun and that's what it should be. And so . . . I'm not going to listen to 'Do this and do that, and you'll be right.' Just to get a few bob. There's no fun in that. And the principle of it, you know?

FINBAR. Ah, the principle of the thing is to win a few quid and don't be giving out.

JACK. Who's giving out? I'm not giving out. All I'm just saying is that the way I go at it, the principle's not the science. It's the luck, it's the something that's not the facts and figures of it.

FINBAR. Jaysus. And do you and Kenny get down on your knees and lash a few quick Hail Marys out before he stamps your docket or something?

JACK. Ah it's not like that. I'm not talking about that. For fuck's sake.

FINBAR. Anyway, what the hell are you talking about? You took Jimmy's tip today, and you won, so what the hell are you talking about? (*To others.*) Ha?

JACK. Ah yeah but . . . now listen because . . .

The others are laughing and going 'ah' as though FINBAR *has caught* JACK *out.*

I'll tell yous. If you won't listen. Right? I don't have a system. And I do. I do lose a few bob every now and then. Right? So I take a little tip from Jim. And then that'll finance having a few old bets for the next few weeks. (*They laugh.*) And I've been known to have one or two wins myself, as well yous know and don't forget. I have one or two.

BRENDAN. You do not. Go on out of that you chancer.

JACK. I do.

FINBAR. I'd say the last win you had was fucking Red Rum or someone.

JACK (*aside to* VALERIE). We do be only messing like this.

FINBAR. What would anyone like? Jim?

JIM. Eh, small one, then, thanks Finbar.

FINBAR. Jack? Small one? Pint?

JACK. I'll have a small one, go on.

FINBAR. Good man. Valerie?

VALERIE. Oh no, I'm okay for the moment, thanks.

FINBAR. Are you sure? Top that up?

VALERIE. No I'm fine, honestly.

FINBAR. You're sure now?

VALERIE. No really, I'm fine.

FINBAR (*hands up*). Fair enough. We won't force you. Give us . . . eh three small ones, Brendan. Good man. Here, are you having one?

BRENDAN *is pouring three glasses of whiskey.*

BRENDAN. I'm debating whether to have one.

JACK. Ah he'll have one, go on Brendan. Who knows when the hell you'll see another drink off the Finbar fella, hah? Come on! Quick! He's all annoyed you're having one.

FINBAR (*to* VALERIE). Would you listen to him?

JACK. That fella'd peel a banana in his pocket.

JIM. Is that what that is?

They laugh.

FINBAR. First time I've been in here in ages, bringing nice company in and everything, getting this. Oh you'd have to watch the Jimmy fella. There's more going on there than he lets on. 'Is that what that is?'

BRENDAN *places the drinks on the bar.*

And look at this! Me buying the drinks and everything! Ah it's not right. What do you think Valerie?

VALERIE. Oh, it's terrible.

FINBAR. Oh, it's desperate.

He hands BRENDAN *a twenty pound note.*

There you go, Brendan. I wouldn't say you see too many twenties in here. With the boys, wouldn't be too often, I'd say. Cheers boys.

JACK. Cheers.

JIM. Good luck.

BRENDAN. Good luck now.

VALERIE. Cheers.

JACK. How did you put up with this fella showing you around?

VALERIE. Ah, he was a bit quieter today.

JACK. Well you're seeing the real him now. And I bet you prefer the other one. We've never seen it. The quiet Finbar. This one comes out at night. You see.

VALERIE. Oh, well I was getting the history of the place and everything today.

JACK. He was probably making it up on the spot. Was he?

FINBAR. Yeah. I was, that's right Jack. That's why all them photographs are fake, I had them done years ago just to fool Valerie tonight.

VALERIE (*going to the photographs*). That's all around here, is it?

FINBAR (*going to the photographs*). Yeah. That's the weir. When was that taken, Brendan?

BRENDAN. Eh. That's 1951.

FINBAR. 1951. That's your father there.

BRENDAN. Yeah. I think your father's in it too.

FINBAR. Oh he is! Valerie look at this. That's Big Finbar. .And that's Brendan's father, Paddy Byrne. This is when the ESB opened the weir.

VALERIE (*to* FINBAR). You look like your father. (*To* BRENDAN.) You don't.

FINBAR. He's like his mother. He's like the Mangans. Now . . . Who would you say that is there? In the shorts.

VALERIE. Is it you?

FINBAR. Would you go on! The big fucking head on that yoke! Excuse the language. That's Jack.

VALERIE. Oh my God! How old were you there, Jack?

JACK. Em. Oh I was about seven.

VALERIE. I wouldn't have said that was you.

16

FINBAR. You must be joking, you'd spot that big mutton head anywhere. The photographer nearly had to ask him to go home, there wasn't going to be room in the picture. Isn't that right, Jack?

JACK. That's right and your dad nearly climbing into the camera there.

FINBAR. He was a pillar of the community, Valerie. No-one had anything against him. Except headers like your man there. (*Indicating* JACK.)

JACK. That's right Finbar. And I'm just going in here to do something up against the pillar of the community now.

JACK *goes out the door at back.*

FINBAR. Jays, he's a desperate fella, that one.

VALERIE. Where was this taken?

BRENDAN. That's the view of Carrick from our top field up there.

VALERIE. It's an amazing view.

FINBAR. Oh I'd say that's probably one of the best views all around here, wouldn't it be?

BRENDAN. Oh yeah I'd say so.

JIM. Oh yeah it would be, yeah.

FINBAR. You get all the Germans trekking up here in the summer, Valerie. Up from the campsite.

VALERIE. Right.

FINBAR. They do all come up – this'd be the scenic part of all around here you know. Em. There's what's . . .? There was stories all, the fairies be up there in that field. Isn't there a fort up there?

BRENDAN. There's a kind of a one.

VALERIE. A fairy fort?

FINBAR. The Germans do love all this.

BRENDAN. Well there's a . . . ring of trees, you know.

FINBAR. What's the story about the fairy road that . . . Who used to tell it?

BRENDAN. Ah, Jack'd tell you all them stories.

FINBAR. There's all this around here, Valerie, the area's steeped in old folklore, and that, you know.

BRENDAN. Jack'd know . . . the what the, you'd know a few, Jim.

JIM. Ah Jack'd tell you better than me.

FINBAR (*pointing to another photograph*). That's the Abbey now.

VALERIE. Oh yeah.

FINBAR. You can see more of it there now. What was there, Brendan? When was that?

BRENDAN. Oh, back in oh fifteen something there was a synod of bishops all came and met there, for . . . like . . . eh.

JIM. This townland used to be quite important back a few hundred years ago, Valerie. This was like the capital of the, the county, it would have been.

VALERIE. Right.

    JACK *comes back in.*

FINBAR. Oh it's a very interesting place all, eh, Jack we were just saying about the, what was the story with the fairy road?

JACK. The fairy road? I go into the toilet for two minutes, I come out and you're talking about fairies. (*They laugh.*)

FINBAR. Ah, I was telling Valerie about the fort and everything. What was the story with the fairy road? Where was it?

    Short pause.

JACK. Are you really interested? All the babies.

FINBAR. Ah it's a bit of fun, tell her, where was it?

JACK (*to* FINBAR). You're going to regret me saying this now, 'cause you know whose house it was?

FINBAR. Where?

JACK. It was Maura Nealon's house.

FINBAR (*self-chastising, remembering*). Oh . . . Jesus.

    They laugh

JACK. You see? That's as much cop as you have now.

FINBAR. I fucking forgot it was Maura.

JACK. These are only old stories, Valerie.

VALERIE. No. I'd like to hear it.

JACK. It's only an old cod like.

FINBAR. You're not going to be scaring the woman.

JACK. Ah it's not scary.

VALERIE. I'm interested in it.

FINBAR. You hear all old shit around here, it doesn't mean anything.

BRENDAN. This is a good little story.

18

JACK. It's only short. It's just. Maura . . . Nealon used come in here in the evening, sit over there at the fire. How old was she, Jim? When she died?

JIM. Oh Jays, she would have been nearly ninety.

JACK. But she was a grand, you know, spritely kind of a woman 'til the end. And she had all her . . . She was on the ball, like, you know? And she swore that this happened. When she was only a girl. She lived in that house all her life. And she had older brothers and sisters. She was the youngest. And her mother eh . . .
.

JIM. Bridie.

JACK. Bridie. She was a well known woman in the area. A widow woman. She was a bit of a character. Bit of a practical joker and that you know? And Maura would say that when she was young she was, Bridie was, always doing things on the older kids, hiding their . . . clothes and this, you know. And she'd tell them old fibs about what a certain, prospective boyfriend or girlfriend had said about them out on the road and this about coming courting or that. And she was always shouting from upstairs or this 'There's someone at the door.' She was always saying there's someone at the back door or there's someone coming up the path. You know. This. And there'd never be anyone there. And people got used to her. That she liked her joke.

And Maura used to say that one Saturday evening back in about 1910 or 1911, the older ones were getting ready to go out for a dance or whatever was happening. And the mother, Bridie, came down the stairs and said 'Did no one get the door?'

And they were all 'Oh here we go,' you know? And Bridie came down and *opened* the door, and there was nobody there. And she didn't say anything. And she wasn't making a big thing out of it, you know? And Maura said, she was only young, but she knew there was something wrong. She wasn't cracking the jokes. And later on when the others were all out, it was just her and her mother sitting at the fire, And her mother was very quiet. Normally she'd send Maura up to bed, early enough like. But Maura said she remembered this night because Bridie didn't send her up. She wanted someone with her, you see. And in these days, Valerie, as you know, there was no electricity out here. And there's no dark like a Winter night in the country. And there was a wind like this one tonight howling and whistling in off the sea. You hear it under the door and it's like someone singing. Singing in under the door at you. It was this type of night now.

Am I setting the scene for you?

They laugh.

Finbar's looking a bit edgy. You want to finish that small one I think.

FINBAR. Don't mind my small one. You're making very heavy weather of this yarn Jack.

JACK. Ah now, you have to enjoy it. You have to relish the details of something like this, ha?

They laugh.

So there they were, sitting there and Bridie was staring into the fire, a bit quiet. And smiling now and again at Maura, but Maura said she could see a bit of wet in her eyes. And then there was a soft knocking at the door. Someone. At the front door. And Bridie never moved. And Maura said 'Will I get the door, mammy?' And Bridie said 'No, sure, it's only someone playing a joke on us, don't mind them.' So they sat there, and there was no more knocking for a while. And em, in those days, there was no kitchen, where the extension is, Valerie, that was the back door and only a little latch on it, you know? And that's where the next knocking was. Very soft, Maura said, and very low down the door. Not like where you'd expect a grown man or a woman would be knocking, up here, you know? And again Bridie was saying, ah, it's only someone having a joke, they'll go away. And then it was at the window. Maura couldn't see anything out in the night. And her mother wouldn't let her go over. And then it stopped. But when it was late and the fire went down, Bridie wouldn't get up to get more turf for the fire. Because it was out in the shed. So they just sat there until the others came back, well after midnight.

VALERIE. What was it?

JACK. Well Maura said her mother never told the others, and one day when it was only the two of them there, a priest came and blessed the doors and the windows. And then there was no more knocking. And it was only years later that Maura heard from one of the older people in the area that the house had been built on what they call a fairy road. Like it wasn't a road, but it was a . . .

JIM. It was like a row of things.

JACK. Yeah, like a . . . From the fort up in Brendan's top field there, then the old well, and the abbey further down, and into the cove where the little pebbly beach is, there. And the . . . legend would be that the fairies would come down that way to bathe, you see. And Maura Nealon's house was built on what you'd call . . . that . . . 'road'.

VALERIE. And they wanted to come through?

JACK. Well, that'd be the idea. But Maura never heard the knocking again except on one time in the fifties when the weir was going up. There was a bit of knocking then she said. And a fierce load of dead birds all in the hedge and this, but that was it. That's the story.

FINBAR. You're not bothered by that, are you, Valerie? 'Cause it's only old cod, you know? You hear these, all around, up and down the country.

VALERIE. I think there's probably *something* in them. No I do.

JACK. Ah there might be alright. But . . . it doesn't hurt. A bit of an old story like. But I'll tell what, it'd give a thirst, like. You know? What'll yous have?

They laugh.

Valerie, top that up.

VALERIE. Em . . .

JACK. Go on.

FINBAR. Ah she will. Brendan.

BRENDAN *puts a clean tumbler on the bar.*

VALERIE. This glass is fine.

FINBAR. Oh, country ways! Good girl.

They laugh. BRENDAN *pours wine.*

JACK, Finbar. Pint?

FINBAR. Ah. Pint. Why not says you, ha?

JACK. Jim?

JIM. Ah.

JACK. Three pints please, Brendan.

BRENDAN. Three pints.

Pause. BRENDAN *works.*

FINBAR. Yep. Oh yeah.

JACK. Are you debating whether to have one yourself?

BRENDAN. I'm debating.

FINBAR. Who's winning?

BRENDAN. Ah, it's a draw. I'm going to have a glass.

FINBAR. Good man, have two, ha?

They laugh. JACK *produces his cigarettes.*

JACK. Valerie?

VALERIE. Eh, I will, thanks.

FINBAR (*pleasantly surprised*). Oh! Good girl.

JACK. Finbar?

FINBAR. No I won't, thanks Jack. Haven't had one of them fellas now, eighteen years this November.

JACK. Eighteen years, ha?

JACK *offers the pack to* BRENDAN *and* JIM *who both take one.*

FINBAR. Eighteen years. Not since I made the move. (*To* VALERIE.) Down to Carrick.

JACK (*lighting the cigarettes*). Jays, you don't look any better for it, ha?

They laugh.

FINBAR. Oh yeah? We'll see who'd look better after a round or two of the fisty footwork ha? And you with the lungs hanging out your back.

JACK. Jaysus. An auldfella like me. Ten or more years between us and you wanting to give me a few digs. Business . . . killer instinct, is it?

FINBAR. That's an eye for the gap. (*Winks at* VALERIE.) Exploit the weakness.

JACK. 'The weakness'? Sure, don't you have a grand little spooky story, about how brave you are.

FINBAR. Ah no . . .

JACK. Come on.

FINBAR. Ah that was only the . . . Walsh young one having us all on. It was only a cod, sure.

JIM. She's in America now. Niamh Walsh.

BRENDAN. It was Niamh that time, yeah?

FINBAR. Ah she was a header. Looking for attention.

VALERIE. What happened?

JACK. This was the brave fella.

FINBAR. Ah, stop. It was nothing.

JACK. This was a family lived up beside Big Finbar's place. The Walshes.

FINBAR. Ah, they were only blow-ins, he was a guard.

VALERIE. Blow-ins like me?

FINBAR. Ah no. You know what I mean.

JACK. Jays, you'll be losing business with them kind of remarks, ha? Valerie will agree with me there now.

They laugh.

FINBAR. Ah she knows what I mean. Valerie's very welcome. She knows that, don't you?

JACK. Ah leave her alone, you're embarrassing everybody now. Jaysus. (*They laugh.*) Tell her the story.

FINBAR. Ah Janey. Sure you have her in a haunted house already! She won't be able to sleep.

VALERIE. No I'd like to hear it.

FINBAR. It's not even a real one.

JACK. Ah, she wants to hear one, don't be moaning and tell her, come on.

FINBAR. Tch. Just a crowd of headbangers is all it was. There was a house out near where we were on the other side of the Knock there. It would have been the nearest place to us, Valerie, about a quarter mile down the road. And the old lad Finnerty lived on his own down there, and his family got him into a nursing home out by them down in Westport. And the people who moved in were the Walshes, your man was a sergeant in the guards, stationed in Carrick. And, like, he was fifty-odd and still only a sergeant, so, like he was no Sherlock Holmes. You know?

They laugh.

He wasn't 'Walsh of the yard' or anything like that. And they moved in. He had three daughters who were teenagers, and he had a youngfella who was married back near Longford there. So the . . . daughters were with him and the missus. And I knew them a little bit because that was the year Big Finbar died, God rest him, and they arrived about the time of the funeral so . . . you know, I met them, then. And I was living on my own because me and Big Finbar were the only two in it at the time. So I was the bachelor boy, and a gaggle of young ones after moving in next door, yo ho! You know?

They laugh.

And around that time I would have been wondering what to do, Valerie, do you know? Whether to sell it on or farm it or, you know. I was twenty-two, twenty-three, you know?

And it was, it would have been about eleven or twelve o'clock this night and there was a knock at the door and it was Mrs. Walsh. And she was all upset and asking me if I could come in, she didn't know what to do. The husband was at work out on a call, and she didn't know anyone in the area, and there was a bit of trouble. So, 'What kind of trouble?' I says. And she says she was after getting a phone call from the young one, Niamh and she was after doing the Luigi board, or what do you call it?

VALERIE. Ouija board.

FINBAR. Ouija board.

JACK. 'Luigi board!' She was down there in the chipper in Carrick, was she, Finbar?

FINBAR. Ah fuck off. I meant the Ouija board. You know what I meant. She was after being down in . . .

JACK. 'The Luigi board.'

FINBAR. She was after, come on now, she was after being down in a friend of hers house or this. And they were after doing the . . . Ouija board. And she phoned her mother to come and collect her. They *said* they were after getting a spirit or this, you know, and she was scared, saying it was after her. And I just obviously thought, this was a load of bollocks, you know. If you'll . . . excuse the language Valerie, but here was the mother saying she d gone and picked her up. I mean, like sorry, but I think it was all a bit mad. But on the way back they'd seen something, like the mother had seen it as well. Like a dog on the road, running with the car and running after it. Like there's dogs all around here, Valerie, you know? The farmers have them. There was a big dog up there, Jack, that Willie McDermott had that time.

JACK. Oh, Jaysus, yeah, it was like a, if you saw it from the distance, you'd think it was a little horse. It was huge.

JIM. Saxon.

FINBAR. That was it. Saxon.

JIM. It was an Irish Wolfhound. He got it off a fella in the North.

FINBAR. Yeah, it was huge; you'd be used to seeing dogs all around the place. All kinds, but they'd be tame, like. Their bark 'd be worse than their bite. So I wasn't too . . . taken with this story. But she wanted me to come down because when they'd got back to the house, the young one, Niamh, was going hysterical saying there was something on the stairs. Like no one else could see it. But she could, she said there was a woman, looking at her. And Mrs. Walsh didn't know what to do. They couldn't contact the hubbie, and would I come down? I mean, what made her think there was anything I could do, I don't know. But she was panicking, you know . . . So I got in the car and we went down. And Jesus, now, I've never seen the like of it. The young one was in . . . bits. They had a blanket around her and she was as white, now as . . . (*Points to* JACK*'s shirt.*) as white as that. Well, whiter because that's probably filthy.

24

JACK. Ha ha.

FINBAR. But I'm not messing. And she wouldn't come out of the
living room. Because she said there was a woman on the stairs.
And I said, what's the woman doing? And she said, 'She's just
looking at me.' She was terrified. Now I didn't know whether
she was after taking drugs or drink or what she was after doing.
So I says to phone for Dr. Joe in Carrick. This is Joe Dillon,
Valerie, you'd see him in the town, he still has his surgery there
beside the Spar. Very nice fella. And I got through to him, and
he was on his way, and the Niamh one was shouting at me to
close the living room door. Because I was out in the hall where
the phone was, and she could see the woman looking at her over
the banister. Like, she was that bad, now. So Mrs. Walsh phoned
Fr. Donal, got him out of bed. And fair dues, like, he came
down. And he sort of blessed the place a little bit. Like, he'd be
more Vatican Two. There wouldn't be much of all the demons
or that kind of carry-on with him.

JACK. Jaysus, sure, he'd collapse. He's like that. (JACK *holds up
his little finger.*) Him and a demon . . .

They laugh.

FINBAR. But Dr. Joe gave her a sedative and off she went then,
you know. And we all had a little drink, and poor Mrs. Walsh
was understandably, very, you know, shaken and everything. But
Fr. Donal told her not to mind the Ouija, and it was only an old
cod. And it was Niamh's imagination and all this. And then the
phone rang, right? And it was the youngfella, the brother who
was married back in Longford. And he was all, that his baby was
crying and he had it out of the cot and he was standing at the
window and there was all this commotion next door. Cars in the
drive and all. That an aul one who lived next door who used to
mind Niamh and the other sisters when they were young and all
this, who was bedridden had been found dead at the bottom of
the stairs. She'd fallen down, and they found her.

And alright, whatever, coincidence. But . . . eh, that night, at
home, I was sitting at the fire having a last fag before the sack,
and, Jack'd know the house, the stairs come down into the, the
main room. And I had my back to it. To the stairs. And it's
stupid now, but at the time I couldn't turn around. I couldn't get
up to go to bed. Because I thought there was something on the
stairs. (*Low laugh.*)

And I just sat there, looking at an empty fireplace. And I sat
there until it got bright. I was like a boy, you know? I wouldn't
move in case something saw me. You know that way. I wouldn't
even light another fag. Like I was dying for one, and I wouldn't
. . . mad. But when it was bright then, I was grand, you know?

Obviously there was nothing there and everything, but that was the last fag I ever had. (*Short pause.*) They moved away, though, then, after that, the Walshes. (*Pause.*) Yep.

VALERIE. And that was when you moved. Down to Carrick.

FINBAR. Yeah. (*Nods slowly.*) Maybe that . . . had something to do with it. I don't know.

VALERIE. Mmm.

JACK. Moving down into the lights, yeah?

FINBAR. Mmm. Might be. Might be alright. Didn't want the loneliness maybe, you know? (*Pause.*) Yous all think I'm a lulah now. (*They laugh.*) Ha? I'm the header, says you, ha? I'm going to powder my nose I think. (*He goes out back.*)

JACK (*calling after him*). Sure we knew you were a headbanger. Knew that all along.

They laugh. Pause.

Yeah.

VALERIE. I'd imagine, though, it can get very quiet.

JACK. Oh it can yeah. Ah you get used to it. Brendan.

BRENDAN. Ah yeah you don't think about it.

JACK. Me and Brendan are the fellas on our own. Jim has the mammy to look after, but we're, you know, you can come in here in the evenings. During the day you'd be working. You know, there's company around. Bit of a community all spread around the place, like.

JIM. You can put the radio on.

Pause.

JACK. Have you got any plans or that, for . . . here?

VALERIE. Not really, I'm just going to try and have some . . .

JACK. Peace and quiet.

VALERIE. Mm.

JACK. Jaysus, you're in the right place, so, ha?

They laugh.

You're going to have a peace and quiet . . . over . . . load. Oh yeah.

BRENDAN. Sure, you can always stick the head in here. Or Jack, or me or whatever, be able to sort you out for anything.

VALERIE. Thanks. I should be okay.

JACK. You're only ten minutes up the road. And Jaysus, by the looks of things you'll have a job keeping Finbar away. Ha?

VALERIE. Ah he's a dote.

JACK. Jays, I never heard him called that before, ha? Lots of other things, never that though.

FINBAR *comes back.*

FINBAR. What have you fecking heard? What are you talking about this time, Mullen, ha? About how twenty Germans were poisoned by the drink in here, last Summer. (*Winks at* BRENDAN.) Ha?

JACK. No, I'd say the Arms is the place where that kind of carry on happens. You'd get a pint in there now, I believe, that'd put you on your back for a fortnight.

FINBAR. Don't mind them, Valerie, they're only jealous.

VALERIE. That's probably what it is, alright.

FINBAR. You see now? At least there's one person on my side.

JACK .Yeah. You. She's only sticking up for you to make sure she gets a lift after you scaring the living daylights out of her with your insistence on spooky stories.

FINBAR. Go on. It's only headers like me get a fright like that, ha? Fecking lulahs.

They laugh. JIM *counts some money.*

JIM. Does eh . . . is anybody?

JACK. Ah no, Jim, I'm grand, you look after yourself.

JIM. Are you sure? Valerie?

VALERIE. No I'll get you one.

FINBAR. Ah, no Valerie, you're . . .

JACK (*simultaneously*). No, you're alright.

FINBAR. You're the guest. You're the guest.

JIM. Will you have a small one, Finbar?

FINBAR. Eh no, Jim. Thanks very much. I'm fine for the moment, finish this pint.

BRENDAN. Small one, Jim?

JIM. Thanks Brendan. I'll eh, I'll just lash a bit of turf on that, will I?

FINBAR. Good man, Jim.

BRENDAN *gives* JIM *his drink.* JIM *leaves money on the bar and goes to the fire, leaving his drink on the mantel.*

JACK. Keep the chill out, ha?

FINBAR. This is it.

FINBAR *looks at his watch.*

VALERIE. Do you want to?

FINBAR. Ah no, no, no. I'm just watching the time. We've a wedding tomorrow.

VALERIE. Would you be . . . directly . . . working in the hotel?

JACK. Saves him paying someone's wages.

FINBAR. Sure that's how I have it, boy. (*He winks at* VALERIE.)

JACK. We know.

FINBAR. No. There's certain things I'd do myself on a big day. One of the first things I ever learned in the business. The importance of good stock.

VALERIE. Soup stock?

FINBAR. For the soup. For the gravy, for the sauces, ah, you use it all over the place. And it's just a little thing I do. A little ritual. In the morning, I help do the stock. What do we have from yesterday, and so on. A little mad thing I do, but there you are.

VALERIE. I think that's lovely.

FINBAR. Ah, it's a little thing I do. Little superstition. These'll tell you. I'm famous for it.

JACK. It's a gimmick.

BRENDAN. Who's getting married, Finbar?

FINBAR. Do you know Nuala Donnelly? 'Nu' they call her. She used to work for me in the Arms. Declan Donnelly's girl. Gas young one.

BRENDAN. Oh yeah.

FINBAR. You used to be pals with Declan, Jim.

JIM. Poor Declan. Be ten years dead in July. God rest him. Lovely fella.

FINBAR. She's a gas young one, the daughter. 'Nu' they call her. 'Call me "Nu",' she says, the first day she was working for me. Not afraid to speak up for herself or anything. Used to tell us who was having affairs and all this. She was chambermaid, you see. She knew the couples who were being all illicit because she'd go in to do the room in the morning and the bed would be

28

already made. The woman in the affair would have done it out of guilt, you see. Cover it all up, for herself as much as for anyone else. She's a mad young one.

VALERIE. Would you get many people using the hotel like that?

FINBAR. Not at all. I wouldn't say so. But Nuala just you know, she's a gabber and a talker.

JIM (*at fire*). Who's she getting married to Finbar?

FINBAR. Oh Jesus some fella from out the country. He must be in his forties. Shame, a young one getting hitched to an old fella like that. He must have plenty of money. (*To* VALERIE.) Be like getting married to that. (*Indicating* JACK.) He's a nice stash hidden away in that little garage, I'll tell you. Hoping to trap some little thing with it. Isn't that right, Jack?

JACK. That's my plan.

FINBAR. But you'd want to be careful of the old lads living on their own. They've a big pot of stew constantly on the heat, and they just keep throwing a few old bits of scraps in it every couple of days. And they survive off that, don't you Jack? That'd do you.

JACK. It's a feast every day.

FINBAR. Aw. Dreadful fellas. And then they manage to get a girl and the dust'd be like that on everything. And your man'd be after living in two rooms all his life, and the poor young one would have to get in and clean it all out. Thirty years of old newspapers and cheap thrillers, all lying there in the damp since their mammies died and that was the last bit of cleaning went on in the place. That right Jack?

JACK. That's us to a tee.

BRENDAN. Jaysus, speak for yourself, ha?

FINBAR. Oh, they'd be desperate men. Changing the sheets in the bed every Christmas. And there'd be soot all over everything, and bits of rasher, and egg and pudding on the floor.

VALERIE. The poor girl.

FINBAR. The poor girl is right. So the least I can do is make sure her reception, in the Arms, is a little memory for her to have in the future, in the cold nights. Cheers.

They have all enjoyed this.

JACK. You've a terrible warped mind, do you know that?

FINBAR (*winks at* VALERIE). Sure I'm only telling it like it is, ha?

JIM. Nuala getting married. You don't feel the time.

FINBAR. No.

JIM. Mm. I remember, oh, it must have been twenty or more years ago, doing a job with him. Declan. Talking about what we were, saying earlier. The priest over in Glen was looking for a couple of lads to do a bit of work. And he was down in Carrick in the Arms. He'd, come over, from Glen. You know? Which was an odd thing anyway. Like what was he doing coming over all the way just to get a couple of young fellas? But Declan Donnelly got put onto him. There was a few quid and he knocked up to me and we were to go over to the church in Glen the following day. And I remember I was dying with the 'flu and I had a terrible high temperature. The mother was telling me to stay in the leaba. Burn it off. But like it was a couple of quid on the Q.T. so I told Declan, yeah, I'd do it tomorrow. No problem. And then the next day it was lashing rain. I'll never forget it. He called for me in his dad's car. The smell of sheep in it like you wouldn't believe. God, it would kill you. He used to put them in the car, chauffeur them around, you know?

Smiles.

And we drove over to Glen. And the priest took us into the Sacristy, and the job, of all things was to dig a grave in the yard. That day was the removal of the remains and they needed the grave for the morning.

And fair dues, like, Declan said it to him. Was there no one else around the place could have done it? And the priest got a bit cagey and he was saying something about the local boys being busy with a game of Gaa, or something. And the rain was pelting down and he gave us leggings and wellies and the whole bit they had there and a couple of shovels. And then he put up his umbrella all annoyed, like, and he brought us out, over to a grave under a tree. It was a family one and there were two down in it already, the mother and the father, and this was going to be for the boy. Well, he was a man, like, a middle-aged fella. But there was two in it so we wouldn't have to go down for miles, like. So he went off to do his business and get ready, and me and Declan got stuck in. And with the rain and all, I was dying with the 'flu. My arms were sore and then my legs got sore. And then my neck got sore. And I was boiling. But we got down two, two and a half foot and we took a break. We got in Declan's car and he pulled out a bottle of poitín. I couldn't eat, but I had a good belt of the bottle, like. Knocked me into some sort of shape.

And we just sat there for a while, listening to the radio, and the rain coming down, and then we got out and got stuck in again.

Having a swig every half hour or so, keeping it going. And we saw the hearse arrive then. And the mad thing was there was only about two or three other fellas there for the service. Of course the removal is only a short thing mostly, but to have no one there, and for a man who's not an old man, it was funny, you know? And then that was over and the priest came out to us. We were nearly finished. And he just cleared us for the funeral in the morning, and then he went off. So me and Declan were the only two there then.

Short pause.

And your man was laid out in the church. And Declan went off to get a tarp to stretch . . . over . . . the grave, and I put a big lump of a door over it. And I was just waiting on Declan and having the last drop, under the tree, dying to get in out of the rain, and thinking maybe we'd stick the head in somewhere for a quick pint on the way back. You know? And then, I saw this, fella, come out of the church. And he walked straight over to me. He was in a suit so I reckoned he was . . . paying his respects or whatever. And over he comes, through the gravestones. And he was looking around him a bit, like he didn't know the place. And he stood beside me, under the tree, looking at the grave. I didn't know what to say, you know? And he goes, 'Is this for so and so?' I forget the name. And I go, 'That's right, yeah.' And he says, 'That's the wrong grave.' And I'm like, 'No. This is where the priest said, like.' And he looked at me breathing hard, through his nose. Like he was holding his temper. And he goes, 'Come on, I'll show you.' And he walks off. And, I was all like 'fuck this' you know? And I was cursing Declan, waiting for him to come back. And your man turns around, you know 'Come on, it's over here.' I just, he was a lulah, you know? And I was nearly climbing into the grave myself, with the tiredness. And I was sick. So I followed him just to get it over with. And he stopped at a grave. Like a new enough one. A white one with a picture of a little girl on it.

And he says, 'It's this one, here.' And I just went, 'Okay, right you are mister, I'll have it done, no problem. See you now.' And he . . . sort of touched the gravestone and he went off, back into the church. I was breathing a few sighs of relief, I'll tell you. And Declan came back with the tarp and I said,' Did you see your man?' And he didn't know what I was talking about. So I told him and all this, and we just kind of had a bit of a laugh at it. And we just got out of there. Stopped into the Green Man on the way back for a few pints and that night, my fever broke. But I was knackered. The mother wouldn't let me go to the burial. Declan did it on his own I think. But I was laid up for a couple of days. And one day the mother brought me in the paper and on the obituaries, there was a picture of your man whose grave we'd dug. And you know what I'm going to say. It was the spit of your man I'd met in the graveyard. So I thought first it was a brother or a relative or someone, I'd met. And I forgot about it a bit and didn't think about it for ages until one night Declan told me he'd found out why the priest from Glen was looking for a couple of Carrick fellas, for the job.

The fella who'd died had had a bit of a reputation for 'em, being a pervert. And Jesus, when I heard that you know? If it was him. And he wanted to go down in the grave with the . . . little girl. Even after they were gone. It didn't bear . . . thinking about. It came back when you said about Declan's girl. Yeah.

Pause.

FINBAR. Jaysus, Jim. That's a terrible story to be telling.

JIM. Well, you know. I was very sick and we'd had the few little drinks. From Dick Lenihan's batch, you know?

JACK. Oh Jesus. Firewater. Sure that'd put a hole in the glass, let alone give you hallucinations.

A little laugh. Pause.

VALERIE. Do you think it was a, an hallucination Jim?

JIM. God I don't know. I was flying like, but it was some coincidence him showing me where he wanted to be buried. And me knowing nothing about him like.

VALERIE. Mm. (*Nods.*)

FINBAR. Are you alright, Valerie? (*Little laugh.*) You look a bit peaky there.

VALERIE. No, I'm fine. Just, actually is the Ladies out this way?

BRENDAN. Ah. (*Short pause.*) Jays, I'll tell you what, Valerie, this is very embarrassing but the Ladies is busted. And with the . . . (JACK *laughs.*) I'm getting it fixed for the Germans like, but I haven't done it yet.

FINBAR. Ah, you're a terrible man, Brendan.

BRENDAN. No, I'll bring you in the house, come on.

VALERIE. Are you sure?

BRENDAN. Aw yeah, yeah, no problem.

JACK. Don't worry Valerie, if you're not back in ten minutes we'll come and get you, ha?

BRENDAN. Jaysus. Give it a rest. Come on, Valerie, I'll put the lights on for you. Out this way.

FINBAR. Bye now.

VALERIE. Bye.

BRENDAN *and* VALERIE *leave by door, back.*

Pause.

JACK. Yep. (*Short pause.*)

FINBAR (*to* JIM). Jaysus. That's some fucking story. To be telling a girl, like. Perverts out in the country. For fuck's sake.

Short pause.

JACK. Like your story had nothing in it, ha?

FINBAR. Ah that was only old headers in it.

JACK. But you brought the whole thing up. With the fairies. The fairies! She's in that house.

FINBAR. I forgot it was that house. I forgot it was Maura Nealon. It was an honest mistake.

JACK. Honest mistake.

FINBAR. What.

JACK. Don't be giving it that old cod now.

FINBAR. What do you mean?

JACK. With bringing her around and all.

FINBAR. What about it?

JACK. Bringing her up the head and all. (*Short pause.*)

FINBAR. Yeah?

JACK. So don't be giving it the old cod now.

FINBAR. What cod, Jack? (*Pause.*) I'm asking you. (*Short pause.*) What?

JIM. Ah boys, we have a small one. Come on now.

FINBAR. Hang on a minute, Jim. What?

JACK. Well you get me to tell a story about the house she's in.

FINBAR. I didn't *know* that though. I told you that.

JACK. Whatever. And then you tell the story about the Walsh girl.

FINBAR. Sure it was you told me to say that.

JACK. What?

FINBAR. Talking about the fags and giving up the fags and all that. When you offered them that time.

JACK. Would you cop on? 'Ghosts' and 'giving up the fags'.

FINBAR. Okay. I'm sorry. What? I regret the stories, then. I don't think we should have any more of them. But that's what I'm saying, like.

JIM. I didn't think. I just said it. With Declan Donnelly and that. It just, you know . . .

FINBAR. Ah no no no. Jim. We're not blaming anybody. I regret it now. And just let's not have any more of them, and that's all.

JACK. Oh, you regret it now?

FINBAR. Yeah.

JACK. It's not part of the tour.

FINBAR. Ah now, come on.

JACK. Bit of local colour.

FINBAR. No. Jack.

JACK. Just don't berate Jim for telling a story after you telling one yourself.

FINBAR. I apologise, if that's what I did. Sorry Jim. Now, I'll say that. But stop with this . . . tour guide thing. That's not fair. The woman's moved out here on her own. For some reason. There's something obviously going on . . . in her life. I'm just trying to make it easier for her. Give her a welcome, for fuck's sake. So don't . . . be implying anything else. I don't like it. (*Pause.*) I've apologised to Jim. And I'm saying no more stories. (*Short pause.*) Sure I'm married! I mean really. Yous are the single boys. (*Short pause. Warm.*) Sure I can't remember the last time I saw a suit on you.

Pause.

JACK. Oh now it's me?

JIM. Ah now boys, come on. That's enough. That's enough of that.

JACK. You think I have intentions, is it?

FINBAR. I didn't know. You're entitled.

JACK. I do often wear a suit. Don't come in here for the first time in God knows, thinking we're fucking hicks. 'Cause you're from round here.

Pause.

FINBAR. Nobody's saying that. You've got the wrong idea, Jack. And it's not worth falling out over. Now, I'll buy you a drink. And that'll be the fucking end of it now. Alright?

JACK. You will not buy me a fucking drink. (*Short pause.*) I'll buy *you* one, and *that'll* be the end of it.

He extends his hands. They shake.

JIM. That's more like it, men. That's more like it, ha?

JACK *goes behind the bar.*

JACK. What'll yous have?

FINBAR (*offering hand to* JIM). Sorry Jim.

JIM. Ah no no no. Stop. (*Shaking hands.*) It's forgotten.

JACK. Finbar.

FINBAR. Ah. I think I'll just have a glass, Jack, I think.

JACK. Ah, you'll have a small one with that.

FINBAR. Jays, you'll fucking kill me now, ha? I think he's trying to kill me Jim, is he?

JIM. Oh now.

JACK. Jim?

JIM. Small one, Jack, thanks.

JACK. You'll have a little pint with that, I think.

JIM. Go on, ha?

FINBAR. Ah good man. (*Pause.*) Jays. That was a hot one there for a minute, ha?

JACK. We'll say no more about it. We might tell a few jokes when she comes back. (*They laugh.*)

FINBAR. Jays. This is it. How's the mammy, Jim?

JIM. Ah, do you know what it is? She's just old. And everything's going on her.

FINBAR. Ah Jaysus, ha? I'll have to get up and see her.

JACK. I was saying that earlier. It would be the time, you think, Jim.

JIM. Ah.

FINBAR. She does be alright on her own, with you coming out for an old jar or that?

JIM. Oh don't mind her. She's well able to tell you what's what. The only thing would be the eyes, but she's the one, I'm always mixing up the tablets.

She knows exactly what she's supposed to be taking when. So. But we have the telly in that room. And she'll listen to that and drop off.

FINBAR. Well that's alright, isn't it?

JIM. Oh she's still . . . I'm taking her over tomorrow to see her sister in the, in the order.

JACK. That's a closed order, Jim, yeah?

JIM. Yeah, you know. They don't talk and all that. But the sister is six years older than the mammy, now, you know, so?

FINBAR. Gas. She'll be alright for the drive?

JIM. Oh, she'll be knackered, she'll be out like a light when we get back.

FINBAR. Ah.

JIM. Ah, yeah.

BRENDAN *and* VALERIE *come back.*

BRENDAN. So this was all the original. Before the house.

VALERIE. Right.

FINBAR. There you are, we thought we were going to have to send out a search party.

VALERIE. I was having a good nosy around.

FINBAR. Wasn't too much of a state, no?

VALERIE. Tidier than I normally am.

JACK. That's he had the sisters over today. That's all that is.

FINBAR. I saw them having their lunch in my place today.

BRENDAN. Don't be talking.

FINBAR (*gingerly*). Oh . . . back off there. Sensitive area. Eh, Valerie, darling, I don't want you to be stranded here with me now if I'm keeping you.

BRENDAN. Sure we can look after her.

FINBAR. Ah no, I'm grand for a while yet.

VALERIE. I, em. Hearing about. All these . . . you know, stories. It's . . .

FINBAR. Ah that's the end of them, now. We've had enough of them old stories, they're only an old cod. We've just been joking about it there when you were out. We'll all be witless, ha? We won't be able to sleep in our beds!

VALERIE. No, see, something happened to me. That just hearing you talk about it tonight. It's important to me. That I'm not . . . bananas.

I mean, I'm a fairly straight . . . down the line . . . person. Working. I had a good job at D.C.U. I had gone back to work after having my daughter, Niamh. My husband is a teacher at

36

D.C.U. We had Niamh in 1988. And I went back to work when she was five, when she started school. And we'd leave her with Daniel's parents, my husband's parents. His mother always picked her up from school. And I'd collect her after work. And last year she, she was dying to learn how to swim. And the school had a thing. They'd take the class down to the C.R.C. in Clontarf on Wednesdays. She was learning very well. No problem. Loved the water. She couldn't wait for Wednesdays and swimming. Daniel used to take her to the pool on Saturdays and everything.

But for such a bright, outgoing, happy girl she was a big em . . . She had a problem sleeping at night. She was afraid of the dark. She never wanted you to leave the room.

One of us would have to lie there with her until she went off, and even when she did, she'd often have to come in and sleep with us.

And I'd say to her, 'What's wrong, when you go to bed?' But in the daytime, you know, she wouldn't care. Night time was a million years away. And she wouldn't think about it. But at night there were people at the window, there were people in the attic, there was someone coming up the stairs. There were children knocking, in the wall. And there was always a man standing across the road who she'd see. Like there was loads of things. The poor thing. I wanted to bring her to a doctor, but Daniel said she'd grow out of it. And we should be careful, just, about books we got her, and what she saw on the telly and all of this.

But I mean, she used to be even be scared that when she got up in the morning that Mammy and Daddy would have gone away and she'd be in the house on her own. That was one she told Daniel's mother. And all the furniture and carpets and everything would be gone. I mean, you know? So I told her after that, you know, we'd never, you know, it was ridiculous. And that if she was scared or worried at all during the day to ring me, and I'd come and get her, and there was nothing to worry about. And she knew our number, she was very good at learning numbers off and everything. She knew ours and her nana's and mine at work. She knew them all.

But then, in March, last year, the school had a, a sponsored swim, and the kids were going to swim a length of the pool. And I promised I was going to go and watch her. But I got . . . I was late, out of work, and I was only going to be in time to meet her afterwards, but em, when I got there . . . There was an ambulance and I thought, like, the pool is in the Central Remedial Clinic, so I thought like it was just somebody being dropped there. I didn't really pay any attention.

But when I got in, I saw that there was no one in the pool and one of the teachers was there with a group of kids. And she was crying and some of the children were crying. And this woman, another one of the mums came over and said there'd been an accident. And Niamh had hit her head in the pool and she'd been in the water and they had been trying to resuscitate her. But she said she was going to be alright. And I didn't believe it was happening. I thought it must have been someone else. And I went into, I was brought into, a room and Niamh was on a table. It was a table for table-tennis, and an ambulance man was giving her the . . . kiss of life.

She was in her bathing suit. And the ambulance man said he didn't think that what he was doing was working. And he didn't know if she was alive. And he wrapped her in a towel and carried her out to the ambulance. And I got in the back with him. And they radioed on ahead, they were going to put her on a machine in Beaumont and try to revive her there. But the ambulance man knew, I think. She wasn't breathing, and he just knew and he said if I wanted to just say goodbye to her in the ambulance in case I didn't get a chance in the hospital.

And I gave her a little hug. She was freezing cold. And I told her Mammy loved her very much. She just looked asleep but her lips were gone blue and she was dead.

And it had happened so fast. Just a few minutes. And I don't think I have to tell you. How hard it was. Between me and Daniel, as well. It didn't seem real. At the funeral I just thought I could go and lift her out of the coffin and that would be the end of all this.

I think Daniel was. I don't know if he actually, blamed me, there was nothing I could do. But he became very busy in his work. Just. Keeping himself . . . em. But I was, you know, I was more, just I didn't really know what I was doing. Just walking around or sitting in the house, with Daniel's mother, fussing around the place.

Just, months of this. Not really talking about it, like.

Pause.

But, and then one morning. I was in bed, Daniel had gone to work. I usually lay there for a few hours, trying to stay asleep, really, I suppose. And the phone rang. And I just left it. I wasn't going to get it. And it rang for a long time. Em, eventually it stopped, and I was dropping off again. But then it started ringing again, for a long time. So I thought it must have been Daniel trying to get me. Someone who knew I was there.

So I went down and answered it. And. The line was very faint. It was like a crossed line. There were voices, but I couldn't hear what they were saying. And then I heard Niamh. She said, 'Mammy?' And I . . . just said, you know? 'Yes?' And she said . . . she wanted me to come and collect her.

I mean, I wasn't sure whether this was a dream or her leaving us had been a dream. I just said 'Where are you?'

And she said she thought she was at Nana's. In the bedroom. But Nana wasn't there. And she was scared. There were children knocking in the walls and the man was standing across the road, and he was looking up and he was going to cross the road. And could I come and get her?

And I said I would, of course I would. And I dropped the phone and I ran out to the car in just a tee-shirt I slept in. And I drove to Daniel's mother's house. And I could hardly see, I was crying so much. I mean, I knew she wasn't going to be there. I knew she was gone. But to think wherever she was . . . that . . . And there was nothing I could do about it. Daniel's mother had to get a doctor and I . . . slept for a day or two. But it was . . . Daniel felt that I . . . needed to face up to Niamh being gone. But I just thought he should face up to what happened to me. He was insisting I got some 'treatment' and then . . . everything would be okay. But you know, what can help that, if she's out there? She still . . . she still needs me. (*Pause.*)

JACK. You don't think it could have been a dream you were having, no? (*Short pause.*)

VALERIE. I heard her. (*Short pause.*)

FINBAR. Sure, you were after getting a terrible shock, Valerie. These things can happen. Your brain is . . . trying to deal with it, you know? (*Pause.*) Is your husband going to . . . come down?

VALERIE. I don't think so.

FINBAR. Ah, it'd be a terrible shame if you don't . . . if you didn't see him because of something as, as, you know . . . that you don't even know what it was. (*Short pause.*)

BRENDAN. She said she knew what it was.

FINBAR. But, sure you can't just accept that, that you, you know . . . I mean . . . surely you, you have to look at the broader thing of it here.

JIM. It might have been a wrong number.

BRENDAN. What?

JIM. It could have been a wrong number or something wrong with the phone, you know? And you'd think you heard it. Something on the line.

BRENDAN. But you wouldn't hear someone's voice on the fucking thing, Jim.

JIM. Just it might have been something else.

JACK. Here, go easy, Brendan, Jim's only trying to talk about the fucking thing.

FINBAR. Ah lads.

JACK. Just take it easy.

VALERIE. Stop. I don't want . . . it's something that happened. And it's nice just to be here and . . . hear what you were saying. I know I'm not crazy.

FINBAR. Valerie, love, nobody's going to think that. But . . . just . . . no one knows about these things, sure, they're not real even. You hear all sorts of old cod, all round. But there's usually some kind of . . . explanation for it. Sure, Jim said himself he was delirious with the 'flu that time. Jim.

JIM. I had a right temperature.

FINBAR. Maura . . . eh . . . Nealon, sure she was in here every night of the week. Brendan. About how much would she drink? Be honest now.

BRENDAN. How much did she drink?

JACK. Have a bit of respect, Finbar.

FINBAR. I'm trying to make a point, Jack. The woman was a drinker.

JACK. We're all drinkers.

FINBAR. But, come on. She was an alcoholic, Valerie. She used have a bottle of whiskey put away before you knew where you were. Sure, who wouldn't be hearing knocking on the door after that?

JACK. Ah you're not being fair on her now. The woman's dead, she can't defend herself.

FINBAR. I'm not casting anything on her. If she came in that door now, if she was alive, I'd be buying her drink, and more power to her, I'd hope she'd enjoy it. I'd be the first to buy her a drink. But I run a bar myself down in the Arms. I know all about what a right few drinks'll do to you. She liked her drop is what I'm saying.

BRENDAN. What about you? And the Walshes?

FINBAR. Look. How many times do I have to say it? They were all a bunch of fucking headers!

Pause.

I got the wind put up me that night. Fair enough. But that's what these stories do. But I resent that now. What I went through that

40

night. But I was only young. And that's over with. Fucking headbangers.

Pause.

And after all that, I'm ignoring the bigger thing, I'm very sorry about your daughter, Valerie, I'm very sorry indeed.

JACK. Oh we all are. Of course we are. It's terrible.

Long pause.

FINBAR. I'm going to have to go, I'm afraid. I don't want to, but . . .

VALERIE . Okay.

BRENDAN. Ah here, I'll leave her down.

FINBAR. But you might want to come on now, no?

VALERIE. Em.

BRENDAN. Ah, have another drink and relax for a little while.

VALERIE. Yeah, I think I'm going to hang on for another little while.

FINBAR. Are you going to go easy on the old stories?

JACK. Ah stop being an old woman. She'll be grand.

FINBAR. Alright?

JACK. She'll be grand.

JIM. Could I get a lift, Finbar?

FINBAR. Of course you can, Jim.

JACK. You're okay for Father Donal's car in the morning?

JIM (*counting money*). No problem. I'll be there about quarter to nine.

JACK. Grand, just, I've got to get out to Conor Boland.

JIM. Yeah. It's fine. Brendan, em . . .

BRENDAN. Naggin?

JIM. Please.

> BRENDAN *puts a small bottle of whiskey in a plastic bag and gives it to* JIM.

FINBAR. Yep.

JIM. Well. Valerie.

VALERIE. It was very nice to meet you.

JIM (*taking her hand*). I'm very sorry about what's happened to you. And I'm sure your girl is quite safe and comfortable wherever she is, and I'm going to say a little prayer for her, but I'm sure she doesn't need it. She's a saint. She's a little innocent. And that fella I saw in the churchyard that time was only the rotten poitín and the fever I had. Finbar's right. You enjoy your peace and quiet here now. And we'll see you again. You're very nice. Goodnight now.

VALERIE. Goodnight. Thanks Jim.

JIM. That's alright.

FINBAR. Valerie. (*He takes her hand.*)

VALERIE. Thanks for everything.

FINBAR. My pleasure, darling. And I'll call up to you now in the next day or two . . .

VALERIE. Fine.

FINBAR. And we'll make sure you're all right and you're settling in with us. You're very welcome.

He kisses her awkwardly on the cheek.

VALERIE. Thanks for everything, Finbar.

FINBAR. That's quite alright. Men.

JACK. Finbar.

FINBAR. I'll see you soon, I hope, Jack.

They shake hands.

FINBAR. Alright?

JACK. See you soon.

FINBAR. Brendan.

BRENDAN. Take it easy now, Finbar. Look after yourself.

FINBAR. I won't leave it so long next time.

BRENDAN. Okay.

JIM. Goodnight.

BRENDAN. Goodnight Jim.

VALERIE. See you soon.

JACK. See you in the morning.

JIM. Quarter to nine.

FINBAR. See yous now.

JIM *and* FINBAR *leave.*

JACK. There you are now.

BRENDAN. Mm.

JACK. I'm sorry for snapping that time.

BRENDAN. Ah no. Sure. I was . . .

VALERIE. I think it was my fault.

JACK. Would you go on? Of course it wasn't your fault. You
know, it's all very well, us sitting around, fecking about with
these old stories. But then, for something personal like that.
That's happened to you. People are, going to deal with it in
different ways. Jim, was . . . you know . . .

BRENDAN. Yeah . . .

JACK. He didn't mean anything.

BRENDAN. He didn't really mean there was anything wrong with
your phone, I don't think.

They laugh a little. Pause.

JACK. It's em . . . a terrible thing that happened. Do you ever
get over something like that, I wonder? I don't mean the . . .
phone . . . call, you know.

VALERIE. I know. (*Pause.*) I don't know. (*Pause.*)

JACK. We're very sorry.

BRENDAN. Come on we sit at the fire. It's getting cold. We'll
have a last one.

JACK. Good idea.

BRENDAN. Give us your glass, Valerie. Jack, you'll have a small
one, for the road.

VALERIE. Can I get this?

JACK. Ah no no no.

BRENDAN. It's on the house now. Bar's officially closed. Go on.

JACK *and* VALERIE *move to the fire.*

JACK. You get yourself in there now. We'll be grand in a minute.

BRENDAN. I'm going to give you a little brandy, Valerie. This
wine is freezing in the fridge.

JACK. Good man.

VALERIE. Oh lovely. Thanks.

JACK. Good girl. That's it now. (*To* BRENDAN.) Jim'll be in a
bad way, all the same when the mammy goes, what do you think
Brendan?

BRENDAN Oh definitely. She's been very sick, Valerie, for years now. Fading fast, like, for years! She still spoils that boy rotten, ha? Though.

JACK. Oh definitely. Oh yeah.

BRENDAN *brings the drinks over.*

VALERIE. That's an awful lot.

BRENDAN. Ah it's not really.

JACK. There's no law says you have to drink it all, ha? Your man does put it back in the bottle.

BRENDAN. Would you ever fuck off?

JACK. I think we should drink this to you, sweetheart.

BRENDAN. Yes. To Valerie.

JACK. Hope it's all . . . (*Raises glass.*) In the end . . .

BRENDAN. Cheers.

VALERIE. Cheers.

They drink. JACK *considers* BRENDAN *for a moment.*

JACK. There's the boy, ha? (*They smile.*)

VALERIE. You've no children, Jack, no?

JACK. No, darling, never married. But I do be telling this fella to be on the lookout. A young fella like him to end up like me.

VALERIE. Do you wish you had married?

JACK. Sure who'd have me? A cantankerous old fucker like me.

BRENDAN. Too right.

JACK. Yeah . . . it's a thing, you know? I do say it to Brendan. I'm down in the garage. And the fucking tin roof on the thing. On my own on that country road. You see it was bypassed by the main road into Carrick. And there's no . . . like in the summer the heat has the place like an oven, with the roof, or if it's not that, it's the rain pelting down on it like bricks, the noise of it. You've heard it Brendan. You can't even hear the radio anymore. And there'll you'd be, the only car'd be stopping in be someone that knows the area real well. Ah you'd definitely feel it, like. But you know. I get down here for a pint and that. There's a lot to be said for the company. And the . . . you know, the . . . someone there. Oh yeah.

VALERIE. Did you never consider it? When you were young.

JACK. Oh sure, yeah, of course I did, sure what the hell else does a youngfella be thinking about? You know? And Brendan knows.

44

I had a girl, a lovely girl back then. We were courting for three years, and em, 1963 to '66. But she wanted to go up to Dublin, you know. She would have felt that that's what we should have done. And I don't know why it was a thing with me that I . . . an irrational fear, I suppose, that kept me here. And I couldn't understand why she wanted to be running off up to Dublin, you know? And she did in the end, anyway, like. And she was working up there waiting for me to come. But it was with me that it was like a mad thing, that I thought it was a thousand fucking miles away. Hated going up. I went up a few times like.

But . . . I was going up for . . . you know . . . she had a room. A freezing, damp place. I was a terrible fella. It became that that was the only thing I was going for. I couldn't stand being away. I don't know why. Ah I'd be all excited about going up for . . . the physical . . . the freedom of it. But after a day and a night, and I'd had my fill, we'd be walking in the park and I'd be all catty and bored, and moochy. (*Pause.*) Breaking the poor girl's heart. Ah, you get older and you look back on why you did things, you see that a lot of the time, there wasn't a reason. You do a lot of things out of pure cussedness. I stopped answering her letters. And I'd fucking dread one coming to the house. And her in it wondering how I was and was there something wrong with the post or this. (*Pause.*) I can't explain what carry on I was up to. I had just . . . left her out. Being the big fella, me dad handing over the business to me. Me swanning around. A man of substance. And then I had the gall to feel resentful when she wrote and said she was getting married to a fella.

Pause.

And I was all that it was her fault for going in the first place. Tss.

There was a delegation of people from all around here going up to the wedding on a bus. And I was just one of the crowd. Just one of the guests. In my suit, and the shoes nearly polished off me. And a hangover like you wouldn't believe. I'd been up 'til five or more, swilling this stuff, looking at the fire. And we were all on the bus at nine. And all the chat all around was why she hadn't come home to get married. And me sick as a dog. The smell of Brylcreem off all us culchies – sitting in the church in Phibsboro. All her lovely-looking nurse friends and their guard boyfriends. She was marrying a guard. Huge fella. Shoulders like a big gorilla. And they were going down the aisle after, and I caught her eye. And I gave her the cheesiest little grin you've ever seen. A little grin that was saying, 'Enjoy your big gorilla, 'cause the future's all ahead of me.'

And she just looked at me like I was only another guest at the wedding. And that was that. And the future *was* all ahead of me.

Years and years of it. I could feel it coming. All those things you've got to face on your own. All by yourself. And you bear it 'cause you're showing everybody you're a great fella altogether. But I left the church like a little boy. And I walked away. I couldn't go to the reception. I just kept walking. There was a light rain. And then I was in town. It was a dark day. Like there was a roof on the city. And I found myself in a little labyrinth of streets. With nothing doing. And I ducked into a pub. Little dark place. Just one or two others there. A businesslike barman. Like yourself Brendan, ha?

Businesslike, dutiful. And I put a pint or two away. And a small one or two. And I sat there, just looking down at the dirty wooden bar. And the barman asked me if I was alright? Simple little question. And I said I was. And he said he'd make me a sandwich. And I said okay. And I nearly started crying – because you know, here was someone just . . . And I watched him. He took two big slices off a fresh loaf and buttered them carefully, spreading it all around. I'll never forget it. And then he sliced some cheese and cooked ham and an onion out of a jar, and put it all on a plate and sliced it down the middle. And, just someone doing this for me. And putting it down in front of me. 'Get that down you, now,' he said. And then he folded up his newspaper and put on his jacket, and went off on his break. And there was another barman then. And I took this sandwich up and I could hardly swallow it, because of the lump in my throat. But I ate it all down because someone I didn't know had done this for me. Such a small thing. But a huge thing. In my condition.

It fortified me, like no meal I ever had in my life. And I went to the reception. And I was properly ashamed of myself. There was a humility I've tried to find since. But goodness wears off. And it just gets easier to be a contrary bollocks.

Down in the garage. Spinning small jobs out all day. Taking hours to fix a puncture. Stops you thinking about what might of been and what you should have done. It's like looking away. Like I did at that reception. You should only catch someone's eye for the right reason.

But I do be at this fella, don't I? (*Pause.*)

Yep. (*Pause.*) I may be on my way now. (*Pause.*)

BRENDAN. Will you be alright in that wind?

JACK. Jaysus I should be used to that road by now, says you, ha?

BRENDAN. I'll get you the torch.

JACK. Am I a moaner?

BRENDAN (*going*). There's well fucking worse, I'll tell you.

Exits.

JACK. Well. That wasn't a ghostly story. Anyway, At least, ha?

VALERIE, No.

JACK. We've had enough of them. (*Pause.*) We'll all be ghosts soon enough, says you ha?

VALERIE. Mmm.

JACK. We'll all be sitting here. Sipping whiskey all night with Maura Nealon. (*Pause.*) Yeah. (*Short pause.*) This has been a strange little evening, for me.

VALERIE (*a little laugh*). For me as well.

JACK. Fuck, We could do worse. It was lovely to meet you.

VALERIE, You too.

JACK. Didn't mean to go on there.

VALERIE. No, please . . .

JACK. Something about your company. Inspiring, ha? And this of course. (*Glass.*)

They smile.

I wonder if being out here in the country is the best place for to . . . you know . . .

VALERIE. Why?

JACK. Ah. Girl like you. Hiding yourself away, Listening to old headers like us talking about the fairies. Having all your worst fears confirmed for you. Tuh. Ghosts and angels and all this? Fuck them. I won't have it. Because I won't see someone like you being upset by it. You've enough to deal with for fuck's sake. I am very, sorry, love, about what happened.

VALERIE. Thanks.

JACK (*standing up*). Makes you feel very powerless. I'll say that much.

BRENDAN *comes in turning the torch on and off.*

BRENDAN. The batteries are a bit weak. Come on I'll drop you.

JACK. Are you sure?

BRENDAN. Sure, I'm giving Valerie a lift.

VALERIE. Come with us.

JACK. Okay, then. Grand.

BRENDAN *is clearing their glasses, going in behind the bar, tidying up.*

VALERIE. Do you want a hand, Brendan?

BRENDAN. Oh no! Stay where you are, I'll be finished in a sec.

JACK *takes his anorak, joking.*

JACK. Is this yours, Valerie?

VALERIE. Yeah right.

JACK *takes her jacket and holds it for her.*

JACK. Come on.

VALERIE. Oh now. Very nice.

JACK. These are the touches, ha, Brendan?

BRENDAN. That's them.

JACK. Now.

VALERIE. Thanks.

JACK. Mmm. Have a last fag I think. (*Taking cigarette packet.*) Anyone else?

VALERIE. No, I won't thanks.

BRENDAN. No thanks, Jack.

JACK. Up early in the morning. Over to Conor Boland. He's over the other side of Carrick there. Has about fifteen fucking kids. Mmm.

Pause.

VALERIE. Will you be in here again soon?

JACK. Ah I'm always in and out. Got to keep the place afloat at least, you know?

BRENDAN (*working*). Don't mind him now, Valerie. Him and the Jimmy fella'll be fierce scarce around here the next few weeks.

VALERIE. Why?

BRENDAN (*stops work and lights a cigarette*). All the Germans'll be coming and they love it in here.

VALERIE (*to* JACK). You don't like that?

JACK *makes a face.*

BRENDAN. He thinks they're too noisy.

JACK. See, you don't know what they do be saying or anything.

BRENDAN. Him and Jimmy be sitting there at the bar with big sour pusses on them. Giving out like a couple of old grannies.

JACK. Ah we're not that bad.

BRENDAN. You're like a pair of bloody auld ones, you should see them.

VALERIE. Where do you go instead?

JACK. Ah, place down in Carrick, the Pot.

BRENDAN (*derision*). 'The Pot'. There does be just as many of them down there, don't be codding yourself.

JACK. Ah no, it doesn't seem as bad down there, now.

VALERIE. That's because this is your place.

JACK. Now. You've hit it on the head. You see, Brendan, Valerie's defending us. It's out of respect for this place.

BRENDAN. It is in my fucking barney, respect! The two of yous leaving me standing behind that bar with my arms folded picking my hole and not knowing what the hell is going on. And them playing all old sixties songs on their guitars. And they don't even know the words.

And nothing for me to do except pull a few pints and watch the shadow from the Knock moving along the floor, with the sun going down. I'm like some fucking mentaller, I do be watching it! Watching it creeping up on the Germans. And they don't even notice it.

I must be cracking up if that's my entertainment of an evening.

JACK. Ah don't be moaning. I'll tell you what. If Valerie's willing to come in and brave the Germans, then I'm sure me and Jim'll come in and keep yous company, how's that now?

BRENDAN. Oh you'll *grace* us with your ugly mushes, will you?

JACK. Don't push it, boy. Ah sure, Jaysus, what am I talking about? Sure you'll have Finbar in here sniffing around Valerie every night anyway.

VALERIE. Ah now stop.

They laugh a little.

JACK. He'll be like a fly on a big pile of shite, so he will. Jesus. That came out all wrong, didn't it?

BRENDAN. It certainly did, you big messer.

JACK. Couldn't have come out worse, sorry about that.

VALERIE. Would you relax?

BRENDAN *is putting his jacket on.*

JACK. Sorry. Will you anyway?

VALERIE. What? Come in . . . with the . . . Germans?

JACK. Yeah.

VALERIE. Doesn't bother me.

JACK. Ah, I think that's the right attitude. You should stay with the company and the bright lights.

BRENDAN. Do you see my keys?

He is looking around. VALERIE *and* JACK *look around a little.*

VALERIE. Sure I might even pick up some German.

JACK. Ah, I don't know. They're eh . . . Are they from Germany, Brendan?

BRENDAN. What?

JACK. The Germans. (*To* VALERIE.) We call them the Germans.

VALERIE *picks keys off the mantelpiece.*

VALERIE. Is this them?

BRENDAN. Yeah, thanks. Are we right?

They are moving towards the door.

JACK. Where are they from? Is it Denmark, or Norway? (*To* VALERIE.) It's somewhere like that.

JACK *goes out, followed by* VALERIE.

BRENDAN. Ah, I don't know where the fuck they're from.

BRENDAN *turns off the light and leaves.*

An Instant Playscript

This special edition of *The Weir* first published in Great Britain in 1997 as a paperback original by Nick Hern Books Limited, 14 Larden Road, London W3 7ST, in association with the Royal Court Theatre, London

The Weir originally published by Nick Hern Books in 1997 in a volume called *St Nicholas & The Weir*

The Weir copyright © 1997 Conor McPherson

Conor McPherson has asserted his right to be identified as the author of this work

Typeset by Country Setting, Woodchurch, Kent, TN26 3TB
Printed and bound in Great Britain

ISBN 1 85459 368 4

A CIP catalogue record for this book is available from the British Library